This book is long overdue.
encouragement to recover[
likely disagree. Anderson exposes his heart as he chronicles his journey from
rigid separatism to a more balanced interpretation and application of biblical
separation. Happily, there are many—myself included—who have taken the
same journey. I have never considered myself to be a radical sectarian, but in the
providence of God, I was born, raised, educated, and involved in ministering
within extreme fundamentalist environments. Ironically and thankfully, it was
in those places that I became thoroughly convinced of Calvinism and covenant/
reformed theology. Consequently, I was suspect to some in fundamentalism and
a token novelty to others. I serve now in a wider, yet conservative, evangelical
environment without a guilty conscience and still believe in biblical separation.
This book is not about my journey, but with its message it could have been.
In reading this book, you may find yourself either agreeing with Anderson or
perhaps beginning a similar journey for yourself.

Michael Barrett, Senior Research Professor, Biblical Studies, Puritan Reformed
Theological Seminary in Grand Rapids, Michigan

This book is outstanding! Chris has written a deeply thoughtful and spiritually
helpful work to help us regain the apostles' passion for biblical unity for our
churches and for our times. The purity of the gospel at times demands the
difficult and painful work of Spirit-directed, Bible-shaped, and truth-centered
separation. But that necessary work is easily diverted from the boundaries that
govern it in the New Testament. Chris speaks to this clearly, charitably, honestly,
transparently, and personally. While not everyone will agree with everything in
this book, everyone needs to read this book. Growing in grace demands at times
the uncomfortable discipline of letting others speak carefully and transparently
in urging us to think deeply from the Scriptures about a topic like this one. Chris
has done so in ways that are both engaging and deeply profitable for his readers.

Sam Horn, Lead Pastor, Palmetto Baptist Church in Powdersville, South
Carolina

Chris Anderson provides us with a book on schism that he was best suited
to write. As he points out, he has made mistakes that he has had to repent
of, and he now wants to spare us similar woes. This is a practical, balanced,
and Scripture-saturated book, which speaks to all of us because of our innate
tendency towards schism. May God help us to read it with humility so that we
may contribute to a wholesome unity among His people.

Conrad Mbewe, Pastor, Kabwata Baptist Church, and Founding Chancellor,
African Christian University in Lusaka, Zambia

Chris Anderson offers a helpful overview and critique of modern fundamentalist separatism that is engaging, readable, and thoroughly biblical. This book is written with grace and clarity—easily accessible to the layman, and thought-provoking and instructive to the gospel minister. It is a winsome call for discernment in uniting around core gospel truths while graciously agreeing to disagree on peripheral issues out of love for Christ, the church, and the advance of God's mission to the ends of the earth.

Phil Hunt, Pastor, Kitwe Church, and President, Central Africa Baptist University in Kitwe, Zambia

This book by Chris Anderson explores the cause and effect of the many sad divisions that have ravaged the church in recent years. In so doing, he allows readers to ponder how this broader conflict is affecting their own spirit within the local ministry context. In a time when American evangelicalism is splintering in unprecedented ways, Chris issues a passionate call that stems from his own fundamentalist background: American Christians should realize that current strife largely stems from a failure to prioritize the gospel. This book is a must-read for professional clergy and laypersons alike who want to understand the grave consequences of schism and renew a gospel-inspired commitment to live in the unity of Christ.

Andrew Bunnell, President, Biblical Ministries Worldwide

Through an honest accounting of his own journey, Chris Anderson holds up a mirror for all of us as we pursue both the integrity and the unity of the gospel. Read this book with a Berean's eye toward what the Scriptures say is so.

Tim Keesee, Founder, Frontline Missions International

I love my fundamentalist heritage. I believe the Bible has specific teaching—often ignored—about when and how to separate from other professing Christians. And yet I also believe that fundamentalism at its historical heart was a movement toward the unity of Bible-believing people under the threat of liberalism. I think I honor fundamentalism most when I do careful theological triage with the goal of having as much unity as possible with other believers. In this book, Chris Anderson sincerely honors his own fundamentalist heritage while bringing its culture and emphases into the light of Scripture. He is a trustworthy and loving help to us in writing this book. Like an old-time preacher, he steps on some toes. He shows us that fundamentalism still has something to give to the church, but also has something to receive from the rest of the church. Fundamentalists are not the paragon of doctrinal purity and holy praxis that we've sometimes told ourselves we are.

Mark Ward, Editor, Crossway

Few things are clearer in Jesus' instructions to the New Testament church than the idea that God wants His followers to be tightly unified around the mission of the gospel. I am thankful that my friend Chris Anderson has written against the destructive spirit of schism and sectarianism that has long divided devoted biblicists and orthodox believers. This book will challenge you with biblical perspective and godly discernment. More importantly, it will set you free and draw you back into fellowship and mission with loving friendships and influences you didn't know you were missing!

Cary Schmidt, Pastor, Emmanuel Baptist Church in Newington, Connecticut

CHRIS ANDERSON

The
SCANDAL
of
SCHISM

A JOURNEY FROM
SINFUL DIVISION TO
BIBLICAL FIDELITY

Published by Church Works Media
FIRST EDITION 2024
Editing by Abby Huffstutler, Joe Tyrpak, and Paul Keew
Cover design, illustrations, and layout by Joe Tyrpak

ISBN 979-8-9873274-3-2 (paperback)
churchworksmedia.com

To Joe Tyrpak, who did more than anyone to help me
identify and address my own schismatic spirit.
Thank you for your patience, loyalty,
and faithful wounds.

THE SCANDAL OF SCHISM
A JOURNEY FROM SINFUL DIVISION TO BIBLICAL FIDELITY

schism /'s(k)i-zəm/

noun

"a split or division between strongly opposed sections or parties, caused by differences in opinion or belief"

"I appeal to you, brothers, by the name of our Lord Jesus Christ, that all of you agree, and that there be no divisions [*skismata*] among you, but that you be united in the same mind and the same judgment."

—*1 Corinthians 1:10*

"That there may be no division [*skisma*] in the body, but that the members may have the same care for one another."

—*1 Corinthians 12:25*

"The word schism comes from the Greek 'to rend' . . . . The true nature of schism is this: an uncharitable, unjust, rash, violent breaking from union with the church or the members of it."

—*Jeremiah Burroughs[1]*

---

1   Jeremiah Burroughs, *Irenicum to the Lovers of Truth and Peace* (Morgan, PA: Soli Deo Gloria Publications, 1997), 248–49. It is not my intent to precisely equate the English word *schism* and the Greek word *skisma*, each of which has its own distinct semantic domain. However, both generally describe an undesirable breach in what should be whole.

AN EXPLANATION, AN OVERVIEW, AND AN APPEAL

"The way of a fool is right in his own eyes,
but a wise man listens to advice."

—*Proverbs 12:15*

I'd like to take up the pattern of esteemed writers like Bunyan and Shakespeare by appealing to my "gentle readers." My prayer is that this book will be a help to Christ's church and to fellow Christians—not a lightning rod or a stumbling block. To that end, let me offer a brief explanation, overview, and appeal.

An Explanation

This book has been in process for several years, and it has survived multiple revisions. I mention this simply to note that I have not written it rashly. I'm not angry. I'm remorseful for the times when I have brought unnecessary division to Christ's church. The failures I highlight in these pages are primarily my own. But I'm also profoundly hopeful that the church can do better. With that goal in mind, I have endeavored to write with charity. That said, despite my efforts to produce more light than heat in these pages, I do say some things that are *hard*. If some of my words are perceived to be wounds, please take them as the faithful wounds of a friend (Proverbs 27:6).

Several early reviewers urged me to identify the intended audience for this book, which will very likely affect the way it's interpreted. I'm writing to those in or from a Christian fundamentalist setting, urging you to retain the best elements of that movement while jettisoning unbiblical extremes. I'm writing to confessional and conservative evangelicals who are rightly defending the faith and making biblical fidelity a test of fellowship, but who at times evidence the exacting spirit and excesses of imbalanced fundamentalists on secondary issues. And I'm writing to the broader evangelical who may be unaware of what fundamentalism was or is, appealing to you to consider the many times that the Bible urges principled division as well as principled unity.

An Overview

Part 1 of this book describes the past, both the history of Christian fundamentalism in the last hundred years and a biographical history of my experience within fundamentalism for the last fifty years—some good and some bad. Much of this section is anecdotal. But while the experiences are my own, I believe they are shared by and may be a help to many others who have labored in this same part of the vineyard.

Part 2 gets more intentionally exegetical, searching out the many biblical commands to separate, primarily from false teachers but also from perpetually unrepentant Christians. The section concludes with a reminder of Jesus' passion for unity within His church—a burden which has been shared within fundamentalism, at its best, historically.

Part 3 argues against excessive, unbiblical separation with an exegetical foothold in 2 John, 3 John, Galatians 2, 1 Corinthians, and the Psalms—including a chapter on the too-controversial topic of Chrisian music.

Part 4 casts a vision for principled unity in the twenty-first century, addressing the centrality of the local church, the need for deference on secondary issues, and the tragic racial division that lingers in Christ's church. The book culminates with a vision for a renewed unity that rallies to biblical orthodoxy and Great-Commission ministry.

An Appeal

I encourage readers from various backgrounds to read with an open mind and a tender heart, rather than just seeking to find fault with what I have written. The argument of the book unfolds rather deliberately, so please withhold judgment until you've heard me out. You obviously shouldn't accept what I propose with naïve credulity. But I invite you to follow the example of the Bereans, who "received the word with all eagerness, examining the Scriptures daily to see if these things were so" (Acts 17:11). Examine the Scriptures, then, and examine yourselves, as I have examined myself. The Bible condemns those who assume that they are without fault (Proverbs 12:15; 16:2; 21:2), and it commends those who are willing to inspect and improve themselves (Proverbs 9:9; 12:1; 19:20). I ask you to be open to the possibility that you may have some blind spots, in the spirit of Psalm 139:23–24.

> Search me, O God, and know my heart!
> Try me and know my thoughts!
> And see if there be any grievous way in me,
> And lead me in the way everlasting!

Grace to you.

Chris Anderson
Grayson, Georgia
2024

INTRODUCTION

FRIENDLY FIRE

"But if you bite and devour one another, watch out
that you are not consumed by one another."

—*Galatians 5:15*

The Bible commands Christians to unite around the truth. And the Bible commands Christians to break unity for the sake of the truth. Both unity and separation can be a matter of obedience to Scripture—or of disobedience. Christians, churches, and Christian organizations must carefully determine when they *must* cooperate with other believers, when they *might*, and when they *mustn't*. It's complicated. Thankfully, Scripture has a lot to say about unity, separation, and schism.

I'm writing this book for three primary reasons. First, I've lived the life of a schismatic, and I want to share how God has graciously been working on me about my sincere but sinful narrowmindedness. In the last fifteen years I've become passionate about the "big-tent" collaboration that can be achieved when believers rally around doctrinal orthodoxy with a missional mindset.[2] As a pastor and a missionary executive, I'm writing to call fellow Christians away from infighting and back to disciple-making.

Second, I've been burdened by the division that is becoming all too common among conservative evangelicals. We are becoming more and more fractured—over COVID, or Donald Trump, or perceived "wokeness," or an endless stream of issues that scream for our attention. I'm weary of

---

2   I realize that the phrase "big tent" is potentially problematic because it is often used to describe political or ministerial expediency that downplays important differences among a constituency to accomplish pragmatic ends. My use of the term throughout this book always includes qualifiers like "doctrinal orthodoxy." I like the imagery the phrase conveys, but the outside border of the "tent" is defined by clear and robust doctrinal positions which necessarily place those who disagree outside of the tent. Mine is a call for those who are doctrinally aligned to labor together—not for a deemphasis of biblical truth.

church splits. I'm weary of turf wars among like-minded ministries. I'm weary of ministry partnerships that fracture over degrees of Calvinism, the timing of the rapture, or opinions about a well-known author. I'm weary on behalf of pastors who are constantly criticized over issues where Scripture allows latitude. I'm weary of missionary teams that break up or leave the field because fellow Christians can't get along.

Third and most importantly, my heart still beats for the preciousness of the gospel of Jesus Christ. If we separate less than Scripture requires, we harm the cause of the gospel. And if we separate more than Scripture requires, we likewise harm the cause of the gospel.

Ironically, the brothers and sisters in my sphere of influence tend to agree on the fundamentals—the big rocks like the inerrancy of Scripture, the exclusivity of the Christian gospel, and the Bible's command not to cooperate with false teachers. But the small rocks—the little foxes, to change analogies and borrow from Song of Solomon 2:15—are spoiling the orthodox vineyard. Every time I see a faithful brother criticized, censured, or canceled by fellow conservative evangelicals, I want to scream, "I've lived in hyper-separatist isolation. You don't want to go there!"

I spent several years of my ministry practicing and promoting a schismatic spirit. My desire was to obey the Scriptures. But I was suspicious of other believers. When a ministry grew, I assumed they must be compromising. When God used someone, I looked for a loose thread to pull. It was an ecclesiastical McCarthyism—a virtual witch hunt. Looking back, I'm ashamed for taking up the role of "the accuser of the brethren"—an office that belongs to Satan (Revelation 12:10 KJV). But I was sincere. I fancied myself a Jude who was "contending for the faith that was once delivered to the saints" (Jude 3). But more often than not, I was an unwitting Diotrephes, elevating myself by blacklisting others (3 John 9–10). It was a rude awakening when I studied the villain of 3 John and realized, "That's me!" By God's grace, I determined to change—to make decisions of fellowship and collaboration on the basis of biblical fidelity, not my preferences or the fear of man. And it's been such a liberating experience!

One of the Bible's most frequent pictures of the church is an army. Yes, the church is also a body, a building, and a bride. But we are an army, and we are in a spiritual battle. We "fight the good fight of faith" (1 Timothy 6:12). We "share in suffering as [good soldiers] of Jesus Christ" (2 Timothy 2:3).

We strive to please our Commander (2 Timothy 2:4). And when the faith is attacked, we go to war for it (Jude 3). While the New Testament repeatedly commands love and unity as distinctive qualities of Christ's church, it knows nothing of a peace-at-any-price appeasement that tolerates heresy and unrepentant sin. Faithful Christians must be willing to fight for the faith. I believe that. I practice that.

But I do have a word of caution for those who are fighting for the faith—especially among fundamentalists and conservative evangelicals, where I'm seeing more and more unnecessary infighting, strife, and canceling. *Be careful. Love the faith, not the fight. Measure twice and cut once.*

While all war casualties are tragic, losing soldiers to friendly fire is especially demoralizing. Sometimes artillery is misdirected and launched against friendlies. Other times, brothers in arms are misidentified as enemies, as when Stonewall Jackson was killed by his own soldiers. Worst of all is a rogue soldier who savagely turns on his brothers in an act of cowardice and terrorism. It's grievous. Soldiers expect danger from their enemies, not their allies.

In his classic book on Christian love, Puritan Hugh Binning laments the church's infernal infighting:

> Our common station is to war under Christ's banner against sin and Satan. Why, then, do we leave our station, forget our callings, and neglect that employment which concerns us all; and fall at odds with our fellow-soldiers, and bite and devour one another? Doth not this give advantage to our common enemies? While we consume the edge of our zeal and strength of our spirits one upon another, they must needs be blunted and weakened towards our deadly enemies.[3]

I am certain that Christians waste too much spiritual ammunition on other Christians. Schism is a serious problem. We're already opposed by the world, the devil, and our own sinful flesh. Western society is becoming more and more antagonistic to the gospel. And billions of people—that's *billions*, with a 'B'—have yet to hear of our Savior. Do we really have the luxury of neglecting those needs while we nitpick at our fellow soldiers about tertiary issues?

---

3   Hugh Binning, *A Treatise on Christian Love* (Carlisle, PA: Banner of Truth Trust, 2009), 40.

This isn't a new problem, of course. Psalm 133 describes "how good and blessed it is when brothers dwell in unity"—which conversely assumes that it's *bad* and *unpleasant* when brothers are at each other's throats. David mourned friendly fire in his own life: "For it is not an enemy who taunts me—then I could bear it; it is not an adversary who deals insolently with me—then I could hide from him. But it is you, a man, my equal, my companion, my familiar friend" (Psalm 55:12–13). Tragically, the same David turned on *his* own friend and ally, setting up the murder of Uriah when he should have been taking the fight to the Ammonites (2 Samuel 11). It all reminds me of Martin Luther's wry comment in the 1953 black-and-white biopic: "The Lord deliver me from my enemies—and from my friends."

Let me illustrate my vexation over schismatic Christianity with an allusion to World War II. Imagine that you're a young American in the 1940s. Imagine hearing that, after years of neutrality, your country is finally entering the war in response to Pearl Harbor. Suppose you enlist, or maybe you're drafted. Now picture yourself being hastily trained, then transported over the Atlantic along with hundreds of thousands of other soldiers. Finally, picture risking your life to wage war—on the British. Not the Nazis. Not Japan. *The British.* Over tea, or the meaning of the term "football," or residual hard feelings over the Revolutionary War. Ridiculous, right? Fighting the British would have been unconscionable when the Nazis were decimating Europe.

Of course, there are significant differences between Yankees and Brits. But the two nations were World War II allies, not enemies. So it is with Bible-believing Christians.[4] Can we continue to fight each other over theological minutiae while the world is being ravaged by atheism, pluralism, and idolatry? Are we not in danger, as Galatians 5:15 warns, of "devouring one another"?

Let's take another run at that illustration to show another schismatic mindset. This time, imagine if America were to send soldiers to Europe to invade Germany—in 2024! We could argue that the Germans were our

---

4   Puritan Jeremiah Burroughs makes use of a similar analogy: "Soldiers who march against a common enemy, all under the same captain, who follow the same colors in their ensign and wear them upon their hats or arms, may win the day, though they are not all clothed alike, though they differ in things of less significance." Burroughs, 146. He later adds, "We have enough to do to contend with the wicked of the world, with the malice of Satan; let us not contend one with another." Ibid., 429.

enemies in World War I and World War II. True enough. But we would be ignoring nearly a century of history during which Germany has rejected both fascism and communism and has become one of America's most valued allies. Times have changed. Germany has changed.

Similarly, there are battles that were fought by Christians in the past that are no longer necessary. Alliances have changed. Theological "maps" have changed. Labels that were useful a generation or two or three ago are now imprecise. Rather than cutting off institutions and denominations based on their former errors, we need to determine what they believe, teach, and practice *today*. If they are doing legitimate gospel work, we should save our ammunition.

Based on what I've said so far, you might think this book is advocating spiritual pacifism within the church. But it's not that. There *are* times when defending the faith is essential, when the fight is necessary, when sacrificing unity for the sake of purity is the only right answer. As Jude 3 tells us, while fellowship around the gospel is *preferable*, defending the faith is sometimes *necessary*. We dare not cower when we are called to contend.

But whom are we to fight? And when? And how can we avoid friendly fire?

I believe with my entire being that the Bible and church history can help us. And I believe the topic demands our attention and may necessitate our repentance. There may be times when this book has you shaking your head instead of nodding along. I may very well be charged with schism as I warn against schism. But it's worth it to me. There's too much at stake to settle for the status quo. I invite you, then, to join me for a biblical, practical, and sometimes autobiographical perusal of separation and schism, all for the glory of God.

◄ PART 1 ►

MEMOIRS OF A RECOVERING SCHISMATIC

"With whom is the Christian soldier meant to fight? Not with other Christians. Wretched indeed is that man's idea of religion who fancies that it consists in perpetual controversy! He who is never satisfied unless he is engaged in some strife between church and church, chapel and chapel, sect and sect, faction and faction, party and party, knows nothing yet as he ought to know.... The cause of sin is never so much helped as when Christians waste their strength in quarrelling with one another and spend their time in petty squabbles."

—J. C. Ryle[5]

---

5   J. C. Ryle, *Holiness: Its Nature, Hindrances, Difficulties, and Roots* (Darlington, England: Evangelical Press, 1999), 51.

CHAPTER 1

THE LAY OF
THE LAND

*"Beloved, although I was very eager to write to you about our common salvation,
I found it necessary to write appealing to you to contend for the faith
that was once for all delivered to the saints."*

—Jude 3

Many who read this book will have very little understanding of terms like
fundamentalism, *liberalism*, and *new evangelicalism*. I certainly didn't know
these words when I began to prepare for pastoral ministry. I'd never heard
of biblical separation, and the idea that Christians would spend so much
time and energy in dustups with other believers bewildered me. I was just a
Christian. Isn't that enough?

Of course, the answer is *yes*. Kind of. The key to your spiritual growth is
your relationship with Christ, your nourishment on the Scriptures, your
active participation in a Bible-teaching church, and your submission to the
indwelling Holy Spirit. You don't need a church history lesson to follow
Christ.

And yet, the recent history of Christianity in the West does affect you. The
issues that caused divisions in the twentieth century are still in play today,
even if the primary personalities have changed.

Suppose you move to a new location and you're looking for a good church.
Let's say you're a Presbyterian. As you stake out a new church home, you
see multiple Presbyterian assemblies in your area, each affiliated with a
larger organization. How do you choose? Well, you need to understand the
difference between the Presbyterian Church USA (PCUSA), the Presbyterian Church in America (PCA), the Orthodox Presbyterian Church (OPC),
and the Free Presbyterian Church of North America (FPCNA), among

others. At the risk of oversimplification, the PCUSA is *liberal,* the PCA is *conservative evangelical,* the OPC is *more conservative evangelical,* and the FPCNA is *fundamentalist.* The same labels can be used to describe varieties of Baptist churches, Lutheran churches, nondenominational churches, and so on. Clear as mud?

Let me give you a quick lay of the land. It may feel a bit tedious at points. But I'm a practical guy with a fairly short attention span, so don't fear that this will be needlessly cumbersome. I want to establish a basic understanding of three terms in particular—*fundamentalism, liberalism,* and *evangelicalism*—in order to define their meaning, the issues in play, and why these ideas matter to Christians today.

To get there, I'm going to describe three eras of twentieth-century church history, especially in the United States. And I'm going to look at each era from the perspective of fundamentalism, both because that's the group I've been a part of and because it's the group that is easiest to distinguish from the others historically. Along the way, we'll learn what the fundamentalists got right, where some went wrong, and how unbiblical schism provides a warning to faithful believers today.[6]

Fundamentalism vs. Liberalism: The Early Twentieth Century

Jokes abound regarding the identity of Christian fundamentalists—the most famous being that there is too little *fun,* too much *damn,* and not enough *mental.* Others caricature fundamentalists as angry evangelicals— and not entirely without cause. But the term fundamentalist was once a noble descriptor that classified noble believers, especially in the early 1900s.

First and foremost, fundamentalists were "Bible" people. As their name indicates, they were concerned with the fundamentals of Scripture. They were doctrinally orthodox, as most of Protestantism had been since the Reformation. But the German rationalism of the late 1800s was beginning to change that. Inspired by the Enlightenment and the newly minted theories of Darwin, German churchmen began to postulate a Christianity

---

6   None of these groups are monolithic, and my attempt to give a brief summary will necessitate some broad-brushing. For example, I'm not accusing all fundamentalists of "unbiblical schism," though I do think there has been a tendency for fundamentalists of various stripes to be unnecessarily combative. It's a fairly systemic problem, not an occasional one.

devoid of the supernatural. They denied biblical inspiration and inerrancy. They sought to "demythologize" the Bible, removing miracles like the virgin birth and the resurrection, denying the deity of Christ, and highlighting Jesus as a moral teacher rather than the Savior.

Most importantly, by making Jesus a mere man, *these new teachings rejected the very gospel*. Scripture teaches that Jesus Christ is the eternal God Who became human in order to save us (John 1:1, 14). It teaches that He lived a sinless life (1 Peter 2:22), earning the righteousness that we lacked. He died a horrific death, not as a victim, but as a willing sacrifice (1 Peter 2:24). He died in our place, bearing our punishment—"the righteous for the unrighteous" (1 Peter 3:18). By taking our sins to the cross and by absorbing His Father's wrath on those sins, Jesus became our "propitiation," accomplishing the complete satisfaction of God's just wrath against sinners (1 John 2:2; 4:10). Jesus' death was a "ransom" that delivered us from sin, from sin's penalty, and from God's wrath (Mark 10:45). This gospel is the only hope of sinners, and the Bible's invitation to all humanity is this: "Believe on the Lord Jesus Christ, and you will be saved" (Acts 16:31).

That Christian gospel was abhorrent to liberals. They decried it as "a bloody religion"—a critique that is still made against the gospel in our day. God is a God of love, not wrath, they postulated. Jesus' death was either a tragedy for us to mourn or an example for us to emulate, but not a ransom. Scripture's gospel that saves people from their sins was jettisoned by liberals in favor of a "social gospel" that sought to save people from poverty, poor education, and injustice—with little or no mention of Jesus' saving work on the cross.[7]

This new surge of unbelief became known as *modernism* or theological *liberalism*. It arrived in America like a theological blitzkrieg. By the start of the twentieth century, virtually all mainline denominations across the United States and Britain were embracing the modernist/liberal theology imported from Germany. Bible-believers within those denominations labored valiantly to defend Bible doctrine. They weren't fighting over music or appropriate worship attire—they were battling *apostasy*. That's the point of J. Gresham Machen's classic book from that era, *Christianity and Lib-*

---

7   David Wells writes, "Liberals said Christianity was about deeds, not creeds." *The Courage to Be Protestant: Truth-lovers, Marketers, and Emergents in the Postmodern World* (Grand Rapids, MI: William B. Eerdmans Publishing Company, 2008), 5.

eralism. The pointed title indicates that liberalism is *not* Christianity but another religion altogether.

Machen's efforts to oppose apostasy within the Northern Presbyterian Church resulted in his own denomination defrocking him in 1936. The willingness of a large denomination to villainize and humiliate a Christian statesman as respected as Machen demonstrated how far liberalism had progressed within mainline denominations. Christian philosopher Francis Schaeffer writes, "A good case could be made that the news about Machen was the most significant U.S. news in the first half of the twentieth century. It was the culmination of a long trend toward liberalism within the Presbyterian Church and represented the same trend in most other denominations."[8]

The early fundamentalist movement was born as a response to modernism in mainline denominations. The fundamentalists were on the right side of this fight. They were courageous defenders of biblical orthodoxy who were willing to "do battle royal" in the defense of the faith. That's not my definition, actually. It was the definition given by first-generation fundamentalist Curtis Lee Laws in 1920: "We suggest that those who still cling to the great fundamentals and who mean to do battle royal for the fundamentals shall be called 'Fundamentalists.'"[9] Curtis Laws and other early fundamentalists called on fellow Christians to stand in defense of the Christian faith.

What were "the great fundamentals" that these believers defended? The inspiration and inerrancy of Scripture. The virgin birth. The deity of Christ. The vicarious atonement. The bodily resurrection of Jesus from the grave. The reality of the miracles recorded in Scripture. The necessity of the new birth. These are not the sum of essential Christian doctrine; the Trinity is a noticeable omission, for example. But these were the doctrines being attacked by modernists at the time, and they formed both a litmus test of orthodoxy and a rallying point for orthodox believers of various stripes.

The fundamentalists labored together to publish *The Fundamentals*, a scholarly defense of biblical orthodoxy that first appeared between 1910 and 1915. In total, sixty-four respected orthodox authors wrote ninety articles, most of which provided a defense of biblical truth against the

---

8   Francis A. Schaeffer, *The Great Evangelical Disaster* (Wheaton, IL: Crossway, 1984), 35.

9   See Rolland McCune, *Promise Unfulfilled: The Failed Strategy of Modern Evangelicalism* (Greenville, SC: Ambassador International, 2004), 15.

onslaught of theological liberalism. Over 300,000 copies of *The Fundamentals* were distributed across the United States. Historian George Marsden commends these articles as "a great 'Testimony to the Truth' and even something of a scholarly *tour de force*...[which] assembled a rather formidable array of conservative American and British scholars."[10]

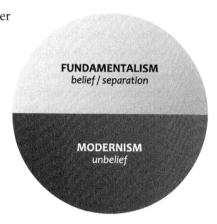

Summary: What Fundamentalists Got Right

There were three main characteristics of early fundamentalism.

1. **Biblical Orthodoxy.** Fundamentalists were committed to core biblical doctrines upon which every true Christian must agree. They affirmed an orthodox creed that included the doctrines modernists were denying. But they also practiced a theological "triage"—the realization that not every doctrine is a "fundamental." They agreed on major doctrines but allowed faithful brothers and sisters to differ on important—but *less* important—matters.

   To be clear, this concept has been embraced throughout church history and predates the fundamentalist-modernist controversy. Writing in 1641, English Puritan John Davenant insisted, "The bonds of brotherly communion ought not to be dissolved betwixt Christian churches for all discords of opinions, but only for the opposing or denying of fundamental doctrines."[11]

2. **Militancy and Separation.** Fundamentalists not only *believed* in sound doctrine; they *defended* it. They were willing to "earnestly contend for the faith once delivered to the saints" (Jude 3). Early fundamentalists began the battle against apostasy by trying to cleanse their denominations of

---

10   George M. Marsden, *Fundamentalism and American Culture: The Shaping of Twentieth-Century Evangelicalism: 1870–1925* (New York, NY: Oxford University Press, 1980), 118–19.

11   John Davenant, *An Exhortation to Brotherly Communion Betwixt the Protestant Churches.* Spelling and grammar updated for this book by Chris Anderson. Originally published in London in 1641. Published online by the University of Michigan. quod.lib.umich.edu/e/eebo2/A37175.0001.001.

heretics. When the fundamentalists lost this battle (as most did), they took an additional step: they came out of their denominations—they *separated*. And they did this at great personal cost.[12]

3. *Interdenominationalism*. Early fundamentalists hailed from a wide array of denominations, including Congregational, Presbyterian, Methodist, Baptist, and others. While they disagreed on issues like church polity and the ordinances, they agreed on the fundamentals. They couldn't have started churches together. But they could and did defend biblical orthodoxy together.

Dick and Rick Gregory, long-time pastors of IFCA churches, give an apt summary of early fundamentalism:

> The militant conservatives had fought the good fight of faith over doctrinal fundamentals and found themselves no longer welcome in denominations in which they were attempting to preserve doctrinal purity. Many lost their pulpits, churches, pensions and friends because of their conviction that true unity could only be found in common commitment to biblical truth, not in preserving denominational harmony. They found it necessary for conscience sake to leave their denominations and start anew.[13]

Fundamentalism vs. New Evangelicalism: The Mid-Twentieth Century

The fundamentalist coalition of the early 1900s was broken by the 1950s, and the breach continues in our own day. The fault line was between so-called "new evangelicals" and the old-school fundamentalists they labored to distinguish themselves from. This wasn't a war with unbelievers. It was an intramural division among Christians.

The *new* evangelicalism was defined by one of its primary proponents, Harold Ockenga in 1947.[14] Ockenga introduced a new breed of evangelicals who would continue to hold to orthodox doctrine, but who would

---

12   Note that both the "put out" strategy that tried to purge unbelief and the "come out" strategy that abandoned compromised denominations were forms of appropriate and biblical separation.

13   Richard I. Gregory and Richard W. Gregory, *On the Level: Discovering the Levels of Biblical Relationships Among Believers* (Grandville, MI: IFCA Press, 2005), 163.

14   McCune, *Promise*, xvi, 59.

also strive to soften their tone and sharpen their image. He called for a repudiation of separation, for intentional social involvement, for academic engagement with modernists, and for a noticeably positive message—all in supposed contrast to the strategy of fundamentalists. Ockenga's was a *kinder, gentler* version of biblical orthodoxy.

Southern Baptist leader Al Mohler gives a rather generous description of "new evangelicalism's" early ambition:

> These "New Evangelicals," as they styled themselves, were determined to maintain a clear and unquestioned commitment to theological orthodoxy and to oppose theological liberalism in all its forms. Yet they also wanted to distinguish themselves and their movement from fundamentalism, which they identified with anti-intellectualism, a lack of serious theological engagement, a withdrawal from social responsibility, and an eccentric list of theological preoccupations.[15]

I would be a little more critical of new evangelicalism than Mohler, if not regarding its intent, then at least regarding what it ultimately delivered. To be sure, evangelicals did erect an astounding number of ministries in the twentieth century, including publishing houses, colleges, radio ministries, mission boards, and so on. We benefit from that evangelical vision and efficiency today.

But the new evangelicals planted their flag squarely "in the middle of the road," in Billy Graham's words.[16] They endeavored to maintain their orthodox theology, but they did *not* "oppose theological liberalism in all its forms," to quote Mohler. Rather, they refused to separate from heretics. In fact, new evangelicals seemed more intent on distinguishing themselves from fundamentalists than from modernists. In the words of Machen a generation earlier, they became "indifferentists" and "theological pacifists."[17] Dick and Rick Gregory write, "The Neo-Evangelicals were committed to finding areas of agreement and cooperation with professed

15   R. Albert Mohler, Jr., "Confessional Evangelicalism" in *Four Views on the Spectrum of Evangelicalism*, ed. Andrew David Naselli and Collin Hansen (Grand Rapids, MI: Zondervan, 2011), 72.

16   George M. Marsden, *Reforming Fundamentalism: Fuller Seminary and the New Evangelicalism* (Grand Rapids, MI: William B. Eerdmans Publishing Company, 1987), 158. The "middle of the road" quote is from a letter from Billy Graham sent to Harold Lindsell.

17   J. Gresham Machen. *Christianity and Liberalism* (Grand Rapids, MI: William B. Eerdmans Publishing Company, 2009), 42 and 147.

theological liberals. This approach legitimized liberals as genuine Christians even though they openly denied the great fundamentals of the faith."[18]

The new evangelicals' cooperation with those who denied the gospel wasn't just an unfortunate misstep. It was seen by fundamentalists as spiritual treason. Kevin Bauder, a respected spokesman for fundamentalism, writes, "The gospel functions as the boundary of Christian fellowship…. Those who deny the gospel are to be excluded from Christian fellowship."[19] The new evangelicals' decision forced fundamentalists to halt cooperation with them—not that the fundamentalists' cooperation was wanted.

Time prevents me from going into great detail regarding mid-twentieth-century new evangelicals, but their refusal to separate from apostasy—seen mostly clearly in Billy Graham's partnership with religious leaders who denied the fundamentals of the Christian faith and in the doctrinal deviance of new evangelicalism's flagship school, Fuller Theological Seminary—was an error that hounded broad evangelicalism in the latter half of the twentieth century and into the twenty-first.[20]

Fundamentalists responded to the compromise of the new evangelicals by separating from them as well as from the apostates. The idea—which regrettably came to be known as *second-degree separation*—was that if *you* cooperate with a heretic, I won't cooperate with *you*. The idea was sound, but it went to seed.

---

18   Gregory and Gregory, 68–69.

19   Kevin T. Bauder, "Fundamentalism" in *Four Views on the Spectrum of Evangelicalism*, ed. Andrew David Naselli and Collin Hansen (Grand Rapids, MI: Zondervan, 2011), 29, 31.

20   For a thorough study on what I deem to be the failed infiltration strategy of new evangelicalism, see George Marsden's book, *Reforming Fundamentalism: Fuller Seminary and the New Evangelicalism*; Iain Murray's book, *Evangelicalism Divided: A Record of Crucial Change in the Years 1950 to 2000*; Rolland McCune's book, *Promise Unfulfilled: The Failed Strategy of Modern Evangelicalism*; and Ernest Pickering's book, *Biblical Separation: The Struggle for a Pure Church*.

Summary: What Fundamentalism Got Mostly Right

1. The fundamentalists were right to reject new evangelicalism's "indifferentist" approach to theological liberals—what Francis Schaeffer repeatedly calls "accommodation."[21] The desire of early new evangelicals to retain orthodoxy while holding hands with heterodoxy proved to be challenging precisely because it was unbiblical. The separatism of the fundamentalists from both apostates and those who aided and abetted them was justified.

2. And yet, the critique of new evangelicals against fundamentalists in the 1950s and beyond wasn't entirely wrongheaded. Fundamentalists *did* tend to turn separation into isolation. They opposed the culture, but they didn't try to improve it with biblical truth. They were so afraid of compromise that they withdrew into an echo chamber, trusting only other fundamentalists—and sometimes distrusting even each other. They seemed more intent on taking the fight to evangelicals than to liberals.[22] They began emphasizing the wrong things. Ironically, like the new evangelicals, fundamentalists' blind spots would prove to be devastating in the late twentieth and early twenty-first centuries.

Fundamentalism vs. Fundamentalism: The Late Twentieth Century and Today

Sadly, whereas fundamentalists were right to combat apostasy (modernists) and to separate from compromise (new evangelicals), many drifted from a healthy defense of the truth into a schismatic spirit. They increasingly treated other evangelicals less like erring brothers and more like enemies. They began focusing on cultural issues rather than doctrinal issues—from communism to clothing styles, from movies to music. Their standards of holiness became external, sometimes morphing into legalism—the unbib-

---

21   Schaeffer, 37.

22   Some fundamentalists have attempted to highlight differences between themselves and prominent conservative evangelicals like John MacArthur, Al Mohler, Mark Dever, Wayne Grudem, and John Piper. But it is historically inaccurate to call these men (and others like them) "new evangelicals." None of these men tolerates apostasy, practices ecumenical evangelism, or repudiates biblical separation. Indeed, all of them have fought unbelief with the zeal of the early fundamentalists. The positions and arguments of conservative evangelical Al Mohler and fundamentalist Kevin Bauder are nearly indistinguishable in the book *Four Views on the Spectrum of Evangelicalism*, ed. Andrew David Naselli and Collin Hansen (Grand Rapids, MI: Zondervan, 2011).

lical belief that we can earn God's favor by our performance.[23] And they began infighting, equating contentiousness over turf to contending for the truth. They failed to rejoice when evangelicals won doctrinal battles and when erring brothers repented. In many cases, they just became mean, and what had once been a biblically robust and heroic movement fractured through continual fault-finding and infighting.

A hallmark of fundamentalists has been an emphasis on biblical holiness. They rightly emphasize the need for holy living, as Scripture repeatedly commands (1 Peter 1:15–16). However, fundamentalists too often pursued biblical holiness through unbiblical asceticism. Many adopted unnecessarily backwards standards and created an eccentric subculture. Men had to have very short hair and often had to be clean-shaven. I was once forbidden to wear a braided belt because it was deemed worldly. Secular music was wicked, and Christian music with a beat was even worse. The King James Version was elevated as the only reliable Bible, often with heretical arguments and conclusions. The use or sale of alcohol was grounds for church discipline.[24] Interracial marriage was forbidden as a contribution to the "one world order"—a racist and biblically indefensible position. Other taboos included cardplaying, dancing, movies, television, and "mixed bathing"—a prohibition that baffled me until I realized that it referred to men and women *swimming* together.[25]

---

23   To be clear, conservatism isn't legalism, nor is striving for Spirit-enabled holiness, which is biblically essential. But it is easy to slip from helpful habits and standards of behavior into a performance-based attempt to please God.

24   I will cite alcohol a few times in the book as an example of an issue which is unnecessarily divisive. My intent is *not* to encourage those who take a teetotaler position to start to drink. Rather, my goal as a pastor has been to conscientiously avoid going beyond the bounds of Scripture and to address the issue with interpretive integrity. In the Old Testament, wine is listed as a *blessing* (Genesis 27:28; Deuteronomy 7:12–13; Psalm 104:15; Proverbs 3:9–10)—but with a *warning* (Genesis 9:21; Proverbs 20:1; 21:17; Isaiah 5:22). Indeed, wine was used in worship (Exodus 29:40; Numbers 15:5, 7, 10) and as a symbol of salvation (Isaiah 55:1; Proverbs 9:1–5). The blessing/warning theme continues in the New Testament, where wine is not condemned (Matthew 9:17; Luke 5:38–39; John 2:1–11), but drunkenness is (Galatians 5:21; Ephesians 5:18). The fact that Jesus made and apparently consumed wine should give us pause about blacklisting it (Luke 7:33–34; 22:14–21). I preached John 2 and told Tri-County Bible Church (when I pastored there in Ohio) that if Jesus couldn't be a member of our church, we've got a problem. It's fine not to drink. It's certainly safe. But we shouldn't press onto the conscience of others restrictions which Scripture doesn't, and we certainly should think twice about making extrabiblical restrictions a condition for church membership or a cause for church discipline.

25   Pastor David Deets laments his childhood church, which "worshiped King James more than King Jesus, measured the length of girls' skirts and men's hair more than our growth in Christlikeness, and was more concerned with what we did for Christ rather than what Christ had done for us." David Deets, "Defending Orthodox Doctrine: A Call to Arms" in *Fight the Good Fight: Reclaiming Biblical Fundamentalism*, ed. Richard P. Bargas (Grand Rapids, MI: IFCA Press, 2024), 64.

Women especially bore the brunt of the legalistic rules. Many were forbidden to wear pants—even when wearing a skirt was shockingly inappropriate or immodest. (Think of culottes and young ladies wearing loose-fitting skirts over their ski bibs.) Speaking of skirts, there were times when it seemed that wearing something frumpy was considered the fast track to holiness.

An interesting subset of the fundamentalists' mindset—or at least of asceticism and exaggerated separatism—was a weaponized conservatism often associated with adherents to the teaching of Bill Gothard, a popular fundamentalist speaker. These families were often suspicious of grocery stores, hospitals, immunizations, higher education (especially for girls), and even of home mortgages. All too often it became apparent that they were also suspicious of the church. Sadly, I've seen seemingly perfect children from these families bolt for the world once they turned eighteen—and more than once I've seen their mothers bolt, as well.

FUNDAMENTALISM
belief / schism

NEW EVANGELICALISM
belief / cooperation

MODERNISM
unbelief

Some will argue that what I've described wasn't mainstream fundamentalism. And I agree that there are certainly healthier fundamentalist streams. But while some fundamentalists may have been more balanced, the issues listed above were more normal than exceptional. Fundamentalism started well, but it too often curled in on itself, twisting the Scriptures in the process.

Fundamentalism's desire for holiness is a good thing—a pursuit every Christian should prioritize. I grew in the faith in fundamentalist institutions and churches, and I'm grateful. But we must pursue holiness with an open Bible and in the power of the Holy Spirit—not merely through rules, standards, and habits. And fundamentalists haven't always gotten this right. As John Owen writes, "Mortification [of sin] from a self-strength, carried on by ways of self-invention, unto the end of a self-righteousness, is the soul and substance of all false religion in the world."[26]

---

26   John Owen, *The Mortification of Sin* (Fearn, Ross-shire, UK: Christian Focus, 1996), 23.

Summary: Where Many Fundamentalists Went Wrong

The early fundamentalists were right, both in their battle with theological liberals and in their disagreement with new evangelicals. So how did many fundamentalists get off course?

1. Some fell in love with the fight. Like soldiers returning home from a war zone, some had a hard time turning the aggression off. As a result, they fought the wrong people over the wrong issues. Conflict became the norm. Francis Schaeffer, while calling on Christians to draw lines and fight necessary battles against apostasy, warns, "Beware of the habits we learn in controversy."[27]

2. Many transitioned from battling over fundamental doctrines to bickering over cultural preferences. Whereas the movement formed by rallying to theological essentials, it began to emphasize things like music styles, clothing choices, and Bible versions. *Fundamentalists* were becoming *peripheralists*.

3. Many failed to exercise doctrinal triage. Whereas their forebears locked arms over core doctrines while agreeing to disagree on lesser matters, many second and third generations of fundamentalists seemed to make every issue a hill to die on. Fundamentalism at its best fought against heresy. But at its worst it fought over hairstyles.

4. Finally, some protected turf while pretending to protect truth. Skirmishes with new evangelicals—and often with other fundamentalists—were sometimes merely about preserving power and obtaining market share. This problem isn't unique to fundamentalists, but it became common.

Once again, the Gregorys provide a helpful synopsis:

Fundamentalism became a recognizable movement as an enemy of apostate liberalism. But the militant spirit that characterized many was destined to lead to further conflicts among those who identified themselves as Fundamentalists....

Fundamentalists, by and large, withdrew [from popular culture] and developed a fortress mentality in response to the tumultuous 1960s.

---

27   Schaeffer, 85.

Emphasis was placed on personal separation from anything that would identify a believer with the worldly culture. Standards that were once a matter of personal choice became tests of spirituality and conditions of fellowship. Length of hair for men and length of skirts for women became indications of one's commitment to Christ. As the world's musical tastes began to invade the Church, music standards were strictly imposed and worship styles were carefully guarded. The emphasis on personal separation and the pursuit of personal holiness were legitimate concerns in light of the deteriorating culture. But the tendency to extremes caused some to develop an attitude of superiority. They elevated a list of external standards to become the means of evaluating a person's heart. The problem was that the external standards were often determined by the culture rather than by the Word of God. This expression of Fundamentalism became tainted with characteristics of legalism....

Separation had become a doctrine in itself and took on a new dimension, extending its principles beyond doctrinal purity to include relationships with those with whom one disagreed. Second and third degree separation became tests of fellowship and obedience. Separatism began to implode upon itself until those who were once proud to be called separatists began to avoid the label because of the baggage it carried. Many succumbed to the intimidation of others, and conformity without inner conviction produced a pseudo-spirituality that was fraught with suspicion."[28]

Understanding this history is important, not only for pastors and seminarians, but for Christians intent on making wise decisions in an increasingly wicked and confusing world. Separating from false teachers, avoiding unbiblical compromise, and guarding against legalism is as important today as in the previous century. To wisely advance into the future requires that we know where we are and how we got here.

Now that we've defined terms, let me share a bit more of my story.

---

28   Gregory and Gregory, 163, 170–71.

CHAPTER 2

"HE TAKES A GOOD STAND"

"I appeal to you, brothers, to watch out for those who cause divisions and create obstacles contrary to the doctrine that you have been taught; avoid them. For such persons do not serve our Lord Christ, but their own appetites, and by smooth talk and flattery they deceive the hearts of the naive."

—Romans 16:17–18

"My name is Chris, and I'm a fundamentalist."

It's true—as long as you let me explain what I mean. I'm committed to teaching and defending the fundamentals of the faith. I believe in and practice separation from false teachers. I strive to obey the Scriptures, not just study and teach them. But for seasons of my life, I was a schismatic legalist, as well.

If you wonder about my "fundie" credentials, I have two degrees from Bob Jones University and a Doctor of Ministry degree from The Master's Seminary—both of which are well-known for their strong stands within fundamentalism and conservative evangelicalism. I grew up in a pastor's home, and I attended conservative (IFCA) churches throughout my childhood. I have pastored two churches that were home to well over one hundred Christian college students and alumni. For a time, I was a member of the Ohio Bible Fellowship, a network of churches and pastors that separated from the IFCA in 1968 and that has had as its primary emphasis the doctrine of separation. Add to that the fact that I've written scores of blog posts highlighting the missteps of fellow believers. I check all the boxes. *"If anyone else thinks he has reason to call himself a fundamental-*

ist, I have more: of the tribe of Independent Baptists; a separatist of the separatists; as to zeal, persecuting everybody."

As I merged fundamentalism with blogging—a combo I called *flogging*—my hypercritical spirit grew. In one sense, my blog "My Two Cents" helped me find my voice as a writer. This was good. But it also created in me an unhealthy hunger for a "scoop." The best way to get a ton of reads was to write something controversial, and the perpetual search for dirt fed my schismatic spirit. I was too willing to rebuke fellow believers, and I was too quick to rejoice in their errors. Thankfully, the Lord dealt kindly with me. I actually formed a friendship with Bob Kauflin after blowing up his church for hosting a performance of a Broadway musical. Similarly, I became friends with Carl Trueman after publicly chastising him over a blog post he made admiring a rock band. Whatever you might think of those types of situations, it really wasn't my business to attack them online. Both men were more gracious than I deserved.

When author Bruce Wilkinson had to close an African orphanage for lack of funds, I mocked him for not correctly utilizing his own tips from his book *The Prayer of Jabez*. A friend, Wendy Alsup, called me out on it, asking if I really found it funny that these children would no longer have the care they desperately needed. Her reproof hit its mark, and I'm grateful for her faithful wounds.[29] I—like others who devote themselves to exposés and "discernment ministries"—put my own heart at risk by taking pleasure in fault-finding.

Now, I realize that the way I initially introduced myself sounds like I'm facing a room full of people in a twelve-step recovery program. I'm still a fundamentalist, at least based on the historical definition of early fundamentalists given in the prior chapter. But I rarely use the term anymore; it has so much baggage that it's become unhelpful. Just call me a Bible-teaching, gospel-centered Christian. But whatever your pedigree—whether you have roots in fundamentalism, conservative evangelicalism, or some version of broader Christendom—we all face the same challenge, which is basically the point of this book: *It is essential that we separate when Scripture commands it and that we don't separate when Scripture doesn't.*

---

29   In God's almost comedic providence, Wendy and I are now on the board of an African orphanage in the Central African Republic called Jonathan's House. Learn more at jonathanshouse.org.

I've not always been the best at distinguishing between those two scenarios, unfortunately. For around twenty years—roughly during college, seminary, and my early pastoral ministry—I would have said, "I'm a fundamentalist and not an evangelical." Of course, I embraced the *evangel*—the good news of Jesus' finished work on behalf of helpless sinners (1 Corinthians 15:3–4). But I identified two binary groups among Bible-believing Christians: fundamentalists (*us*, from my perspective) and evangelicals (*them*, from my perspective). And evangelicals were villains.

As discussed in the previous chapter, I would have defined *fundamentalists* as Protestant, Bible-believing Christians who are willing to "do battle royal" in the defense of the faith. If that's what someone means by the term *fundamentalist*, I'll wear it proudly. I'm still *that*. I embraced the biblical doctrine of separation from apostasy early in my ministry, and I embrace it now.

The difference—where I believe I was mistaken—was in the *application* of biblical principles of separation. I was right to separate from false teachers and from habitually disobedient believers. But I assigned people to the latter category with an arrogant and imprecise eagerness. Imagine a hospital with billboard advertisements all over your town boasting, "We're the leading amputation hospital in the region!" That was me. Sure, amputation is necessary at times, sadly. But it shouldn't be what you want to be known for, and celebrating it probably won't help your cause. And yet, I wore militancy like a badge of honor. Hard-core separatism defined everything about my Christian experience.

My Schismatic Approach to Separation

If I were to summarize my approach to unity and separation at the time, I'd note several elements. I tended to overemphasize separation, and I was careless in its application. I defaulted toward suspicion. ("Everybody's wrong but you and me, and I'm not sure about you.") I was exactingly rigid with others, so that 99% agreement was treated as *disagreement*, in explicit disregard of Mark 9:40: "For the one who is not against us is for us." I was hesitant to learn from brothers and sisters who differed from me, resulting in the weaknesses that are inevitable in a spiritual echo chamber. I had a profound fear of man that led me to make ministry decisions based on others' opinions rather than on Scripture. I lacked genuine grace, at least regarding everyday Christian living. And I tended to protect turf while thinking I was defending the faith. I was too willing—even eager—to critique other Christians and churches, in part to use them as a foil to my supposed faithfulness.

I had learned that new evangelicalism was largely an error. And again, I still believe that. But the category became a "junk drawer" into which I placed anyone not from my immediate circle. In my mind, everybody not in my camp was a new evangelical—whether Billy Graham, Joel Osteen, or John MacArthur. There is clearly an *enormous* difference between the beliefs and practices of those three men. But I would have said there was no *qualitative* difference. (I know: That's nuts.) Basically, anybody less conservative than me was a liberal or a new evangelical, and anybody more conservative than me was a legalist. If that sounds arbitrary and arrogant, it is. But it's how I thought.

Looking back, my approach to cooperation and censure was basically an "alphabet soup." I didn't need to know what people or churches believed and practiced. I just needed to know their labels: BJU, PCC, the OBF, and the FBFI were good; CCM, the SBC, and the PCA were bad; the GARBC and IFCA were suspect—and probably bad.[30]

To me and many of my contemporaries, kicking millions of Christians and churches to the Christian curb simply because of their church's affiliation was justified—even mandated by Scripture. Never mind the fact that within those groups there were countless godly brothers and sisters who were devoted to the Scriptures and the Savior. There was no room for that kind of sorting. Dialogue—even *talking* through perceived differences— was compromise, after all. Nuance simply obscured hard lines. Better to play it safe, call those who differ *disobedient*, and cut them off.

I meant well. But I was dead wrong—or perhaps "Dead Right," as Phil Johnson once characterized fundamentalists.[31] The only winner of such infighting is the devil.

---

30   To clarify these acronyms, BJU is Bob Jones University; PCC is Pensacola Christian College; OBF is the Ohio Bible Fellowship; FBFI is the Fundamental (and later Foundations) Baptist Fellowship International; CCM is Contemporary Christian Music; SBC is the Southern Baptist Convention; PCA is the Presbyterian Church in America; GARBC is the General Association of Regular Baptist Churches; IFCA International historically stood for the Independent Fundamental Churches of America.

31   Phil Johnson, "Dead Right: The Failure of Fundamentalism." thegracelifepulpit.com/pdf/deadright_ .pdf.

Now, let me make a point of clarification, especially for those who don't know me. I'm not generally an angry or combative person. I have sweet, warm relationships with my wife, our four grown daughters, and my sons-in-law—not to mention my beautiful granddaughter! I have long-lasting friendships in ministry. I'm not a jerk. My point is, I wasn't schismatic because it's a personality trait, although for some that is surely a contributing factor. I was schismatic because I genuinely thought the Bible *required* it. I thought it pleased God. You read that right. I thought *division* was the way to please the God Who lists "one who sows discord among brothers" as one of the seven things He hates (Proverbs 6:16, 19). *Ouch.*

I'm ashamed of how misguided I was. Many who are reading this book are parents. Imagine telling one of your kids, *"You want to know the way to really make me really happy? Constantly critique your siblings. Chew out your sister. Ostracize your little brother. Leave him out. Cut him off. Tell your baby sister that she's not part of our family and that you're my favorite. I'd love that. Nothing would make me prouder of you!"*

That's crazy. I've counseled parents who were heartbroken at the way their children mistreated one another. To believe that God would be pleased by our incessant harassment of His children is utter folly. I'm grateful that God rescued me from me.

So, what changed my mind, at least about my eagerness to cut off fellow Christians? Well, it's complicated. The lessons I have learned fill this book, so it's difficult to summarize them quickly. But I'll start with two seminal events that made me question my position and revealed to me how schismatic I had become.

Two Troubling Moments

The first was a sermon series I heard at a fundamentalist pastors meeting. The topic under consideration was God's holiness, and most of the series was exceptional. The preacher—a friend of mine—magnified God's complete "otherness" throughout the messages. God is unequaled, unparalleled, and unrivaled. He is in a category all His own. He is separate not only from sin (which is certainly true), but from all creation. The series was biblical, practical, and God-honoring…until the last few sentences. As the preacher finished his exposition, he made a startling and sad application: "And this is where we differ from the new evangelicals. *Men like John MacArthur don't value the holiness of God."*

Even then, as an "insider," I felt queasy. The punchline of the entire weekend of messages was a self-congratulatory jab at a conservative pastor? It was wrong on multiple levels. First, it betrayed a self-righteousness reminiscent of the Pharisee who thanked God that he wasn't like the sinners around him (Luke 18:11). Worse, it turned God's holiness into a stick with which to beat other Christians. The doctrine of God's holiness should be the most *humbling* doctrine in the Scriptures. Isaiah didn't catch a vision of the thrice-holy God and say, "Woe is everybody else!" He said, "Woe is me!" (Isaiah 6:1–5). Finally, the criticism was shockingly inaccurate. I've heard John MacArthur criticized for his conservatism, his compromise, and his Calvinism. The man is a pastoral piñata. But charging John MacArthur with ambivalence about the holiness of God was nothing short of slander. A red flag went up in my brain. I knew something was wrong.

The second situation was even worse. I was at another small pastors conference. The speaker for the week was teeing off on worldly music—a category in which he placed even extremely conservative musicians. He charged Ron Hamilton (known in his dramatic presentations as "Patch the Pirate") and Majesty Music with teaching children levitation on their recording *Patch the Pirate Goes to Space*. (The story takes place *in space*—weightlessness, not witchcraft.) It was a silly and schismatic assessment. As you might expect based on that example, the preaching was painful—short on exegesis and chock-full of allegorizing.

But the *coup de grâce* was a sermon during that same conference in which the preacher insisted on courtship (vs. dating) as God's plan for Christian young people as they relate to one another and consider marriage. I didn't care much about whether the man had "kissed dating goodbye." Whatever. The problem was the way he tortured the biblical text to get there. It was the worst sermon I've ever heard. It's distasteful, and I apologize for it in advance. But I share it because it was an essential part of my story and a key contributor to my awakening to the problems of schismatic Christianity.

The outer court of the temple represents friendship, he said. Huh. This should be interesting.

The inner court represents courtship. Clearly. The English words are the same after all. (Eyeroll.)

The holy place represents betrothal. At that point I began to get a sick feeling in my stomach, fearing where he was going with his final point. Sadly, he went there.

But then the day comes, when the High Priest penetrates the veil, sprinkling blood as he enters into the holy of holies. The blood reminds us of how the Jewish bride's mother would collect the bloody sheets from the marriage bed to prove that her daughter had indeed been a virgin. The holy of holies represents marriage.

I'm not making this up. He compared the Day of Atonement, the sprinkling of blood, and the high priest to sexual intimacy. It was perverse and blasphemous. It is the only time in my life that I have walked out on a sermon. I couldn't sit there. I was half afraid that the building might cave in. It didn't, but I needed to express how offended and grieved I was.

Now, I know that poor sermons happen in every Christian circle. You've heard them. Pastor, you've probably preached some. I know I have. And bad sermons don't invalidate a doctrinal position. That's not what I'm saying.

But here's the thing that shook me. I approached the host of the conference—a separatist patriarch, friend, and mentor—and told him how offended I was by the guest speaker's sermon. His answer saddens me, even now, and it speaks volumes about the hyper-separatism and schismatic spirit this book addresses. He almost shrugged when he answered me: "Yes, Chris, I agree that that wasn't his best message. But you know, he takes a good stand, especially on music."

"He takes a good stand."

He misrepresents good Christian brothers. He assaults the Scriptures with reckless abandon. He uses the high priest—one of the Bible's clearest and most vital types of *Christ*—to teach a remarkably lewd lesson. But "he takes a good stand"?!

I know this is an extreme example. But it occurred to me that for some, a person's conservative stance on issues like music and separation is *all that matters.* It covers a multitude of sins. As long as you're on "our side" of the separatist divide, you're okay. The guy was against CCM and big-name evangelicals, so he got a free pass, regardless of how poorly he handled the Scriptures. He was "for us," after all.[32]

And I started to wonder if *I* was actually "for us." I wondered if what we were defending was *truth* or *turf*. I wondered if we were really the good guys. Most of all, I wondered if my habitual contention with fellow Christians was really what Scripture required.

---

32   Douglas McLachlan warns of this kind of inconsistency: "A friend might hold to a peculiar set of beliefs, an eccentric pattern of behavior, or a dubious philosophy of ministry, and at the very same moment be warmly embraced because he espouses a form of Biblical separatism." Douglas R. McLachlan, *Reclaiming Authentic Fundamentalism* (Independence, MO: American Association of Christian Schools, 1993), 140. In such cases, separation—or, too often, schism—becomes the litmus test of orthodoxy...the *shibboleth*...the only thing that matters. Ironically, such thinking turns historic fundamentalism on its head by ignoring doctrinal deviancy in favor of partisanship.

CHAPTER 3

THE AWAKENED CONSCIENCE OF A SPIRITUAL MISFIT

*"I am a companion of all who fear you,
of those who keep your precepts."*

—Psalm 119:63

Take a look at a light switch in your home, dorm room, or office. In fact, take a mental inventory of all the light switches you use every day, whether at home or at work. I'm guessing that most of them are *toggle* switches since these are the most common. The toggle—the little plastic lever that pokes through the plate—can either be up or down, on or off. Simple.

But you might also have a *dimmer* switch somewhere in your home, maybe in your entryway or dining room. A dimmer switch allows you to choose from a spectrum between "on" and "off," either through a slider or a knob. With a dimmer, you can adjust your lights to 50% or 70% or whatever amount of light will best serve you in a specific circumstance.

During my ministry training and early pastoral ministry, I got the impression that Christian cooperation and separation were like a toggle switch: *on* or *off*—and most likely off. But it was a happy day when I began to conceive of Christian unity as a dimmer switch. The fact that I wasn't in lockstep agreement with a Christian brother or sister on every minute detail of theology or practice didn't mean that I had to completely cut off the relationship. I could have *levels* or *grades* of fellowship and collaboration appropriate to different circumstances. I came to understand that separation is a spectrum, not a binary concept.

Kevin Bauder was a great help to my thinking in this regard:

> Christian fellowship is not all or nothing. Within the Christian faith, different levels of fellowship require different qualifications. Individuals may qualify for some levels of fellowship but not qualify for others.[33]

Varying Levels of Fellowship

Let me illustrate what this looks like in real life. I'm not a Presbyterian. I've spent my entire life in Bible churches and Baptist churches. (They're basically identical, but don't tell them so. It's a secret.) However, one of my most valued mentors in ministry is Michael Barrett—now a senior research professor at Puritan Reformed Theological Seminary in Grand Rapids, Michigan. Mike and I differ on some important issues. He's wrong on baptism, for example. (Sorry, Mike. It's my book.) We differ on other matters, including Covenant Theology, church polity, and so on. So, do our differences require us to cut each other off at the knees? Many of our forebears thought so, during and after the Reformation. But no, the fact that we can't cooperate on *everything* doesn't mean we can't cooperate on *anything*.

We can write a book together—and we have: *Gospel Meditations for Christmas*. It just didn't address baptism. We can preach at a Bible conference together—and we have—or swap pulpits with each other, again presuming that we'll graciously avoid areas of disagreement. We probably couldn't plant a church together. That requires a high level of agreement.

Since Michael Barrett and I aren't in lockstep agreement, we can't cooperate in every Christian venture. But we do agree on clearly defined biblical orthodoxy. And so, we can cooperate in *many* Christian ventures. Most importantly, we can count each other as faithful Christian brothers and disagree without censure.

Similarly, I'm not sure that I could plant a church with hymnwriter Bob Kauflin since we differ in our understanding of spiritual gifts. I'm a cessationist, and Bob isn't. But I've benefited deeply from Bob's teaching on worship, his work as a hymn-writer, and his occasional mentorship during my own hymn-writing ministry. He's not my identical twin—but he's my brother. I don't need to warn against him or separate from him. Rather, I

---

33   Bauder, "Fundamentalism," 35.

can *learn* from him, and I have, often. And it was a joy to collaborate with him on "Reformation Hymn," which has been a help to Christ's church.

Unity doesn't require unanimity. Read that again. *Unity doesn't require unanimity.* And so J. Gresham Machen, in the middle of a book defending orthodox Christianity from apostasy, pauses to offer this clarification:

> We do not mean, insisting upon the doctrinal basis of Christianity, that all points of doctrine are equally important. It is perfectly possible for Christian fellowship to be maintained despite differences of opinion.[34]

Puritan Hugh Binning, writing three centuries before Machen, concurs: "Unity in judgment is very needful for the well-being of Christians; but Christ's last words persuade this, that unity in affection is more essential and fundamental."[35]

Although I'm now a bit skittish about the word *fundamentalist*, this is what the earliest fundamentalists who battled theological liberalism in the early 1900s understood so well. They identified a core body of doctrine over which they refused to compromise with modernists.[36] Fundamentalists would fight for these doctrines. If necessary, they would lose their churches, homes, and pensions over them—and most of them did.

But even as they fought alongside each other for the fundamentals, they gave each other space to differ on less important issues. They cooperated "to do battle royal" for the faith once delivered to the saints. But they didn't fight over baptism, polity, eschatology, vestments, Calvinism, or Bible versions. As a result, their makeup was shockingly broad by modern standards. As I noted in chapter one, Bible-believing Baptists, Presbyterians, Congregationalists, Methodists, Anglicans, and others stood side by side, arm in arm to defend the faith.[37] It was interdenominational, doctrinal, courageous, humble, and beautiful!

---

34   Machen, *Christianity*, 40–41.

35   Binning, 12.

36   An insightful and engaging read on theological liberalism in the late nineteenth and early twentieth century in America can be found in chapter one of Kevin Bauder and Robert Delnay's book *One in Hope and Doctrine: Origins of Baptist Fundamentalism (1870–1950)* (Schaumburg, IL: Regular Baptist Books, 2014).

37   Fred Moritz writes, "We must understand that Fundamentalism began as an interdenominational movement. Christians who believed the Bible and opposed modernism set aside their denominational distinctives to come together and lift a united voice for those truths that made up

Candidly, most of modern fundamentalism is very different from this prototype. In my experience, it's mostly Baptist or baptistic. And it is *not* generously deferential on lesser matters—from Bible versions to worship styles. Not all may agree with me on this assessment, but I believe that in our day, the Together for the Gospel conference (known as T4G and held from 2006–2022) represented the spirit of the early fundamentalists more than many card-carrying fundamentalists do. In fact, T4G was a big part of my growth in this area.

Me and T4G

Back in 2006, while I was in the throes of my internal struggle over my schismatic stance, I attended the first T4G conference, held in Louisville, Kentucky. Since I was still a member of a fundamentalist, separatist fellowship, I did my best to fly under the radar. (Ironically, my picture got plastered on the T4G website after the event. What's the Hebrew word for *karma*?)

Despite my skepticism going into the conference, I was struck by the gracious fellowship the four hosts exhibited, despite their differences. There were two Baptists (which seems unfair, but yay for us): Al Mohler and Mark Dever. There was a Presbyterian: Ligon Duncan. And there was a real outlier, a Sovereign Grace charismatic: C. J. Mahaney. They disagreed with each other on important matters. And yet, they agreed on essentials, and they *loved* each other. Best of all, they preached the Bible with earnestness, clarity, and accuracy. All the while, Bob Kauflin led a congregation of 800 in gospel-rich hymns with more intentionality than I'd ever experienced. I loved it! And despite my initial misgivings, I was enough of a church history nerd to know that this felt a lot like the early fundamentalists I so admired.

I left Louisville feeling encouraged, but also a bit confused. I felt like a misfit. I was starting to realize that I didn't fit in with hyper-separatists. But neither did I plan to join the SBC, PCA, or Sovereign Grace. I didn't fit in

---

the 'irreducible minimum' of Christianity." Fred Moritz, *Contending for the Faith* (Greenville, SC: Bob Jones University Press, 2000), 22. Moritz quotes Richard Harris along these same lines: "There was a time when men could amicably differ on issues which did not affect fundamental Christian doctrine and still respect and firmly defend one another. Great Christian leaders of the past were able to respect those differences and yet recognize that the men with whom they differed were still Fundamentalists and brothers in Christ. They were Christian statesmen." Richard A. Harris, "A Plea for Christian Statesmanship," The Challenge, December 1997, 1. It is a return to this generous spirit which I am advocating—sans the moniker fundamentalist.

anywhere, it seemed. And that was okay. It pushed me toward a position I now relish: *I could enjoy fellowship with like-minded Christians and ministries on the basis of like precious faith, regardless of their denominational or historic affiliations.* In time, I learned that there are tons of others like me—a whole island of "misfit toys," if you will. My people!

More and more influences caused me to rethink my cavalier approach to separation. I began to look objectively at the ministries of men like John MacArthur, Al Mohler, and John Piper—the men I had looked down upon.[38] The more I listened to their preaching, read their books, and learned about their doing "battle royal" for the Christian faith, the notion that they were compromising on Bible doctrine became more obviously outrageous. In truth, they were "contending for the faith"—essential Bible doctrines—even as my friends and I were taking potshots at them for nonsensical issues like having a drum set on the platform. I was all too willing to critique "the man in the arena" from the safety of my seat in the stands. My conscience was pricked. I hadn't only been mistaken; I had been slanderous at times. I was schismatic.

Over time, I reached a decision. I would certainly continue to practice biblical separation. I wouldn't cooperate with those who deny the essentials of the Christian faith or the exclusivity of the Christian gospel. Nor would I fellowship with brothers who aid and abet heretics. My stance on those true fundamentals was the same as ever. But I was *done* cutting myself off from others who believed and defended the same faith that I hold dear. By God's grace, I was finished with unnecessary division. I was determined to make separation vs. cooperation a matter of *biblical fidelity*—not the fear of man, market share, or outdated categories. I was learning to live out Psalm 119:63: "I am a companion of *all* who fear you"—not just my small clique. If that made me a misfit, so be it.

Now, perhaps you think it's foolish that it took me thirty-five birthdays to learn this lesson. I won't argue with you. But I did learn, eventually, and it

---

38   Here are examples of these men's efforts to defend biblical orthodoxy: John MacArthur's passion for expository preaching and bold teaching against easy-believism and unbiblical charismatism; Al Mohler's heroic efforts to rescue the Southern Baptist Theological Seminary from theological liberalism; John Piper's opposition to Open Theism, the New Perspective on Paul, and threats to biblical manhood and womanhood. Another interesting case study is Francis A. Schaeffer. Though critical of cultural fundamentalists, he was unyielding in his opposition to theological liberalism and ecumenism, his defense of biblical inerrancy, and his critique of what he calls evangelical "accommodation" of unbiblical worldviews. See *The Great Evangelical Disaster* (Wheaton, IL: Crossway, 1984).

has made the last decade and a half much more joyful and fruitful. If I can help others sort through similar issues, I will rejoice.

I needed some good medicine. Perhaps you do, too. Read on.

CHAPTER 4

GOOD MEDICINE: ANTIDOTES TO THE SCANDAL OF SCHISM

"The fear of man lays a snare, but whoever trusts in the LORD is safe."

—*Proverbs 29:25*

I was a schismatic during my early years in pastoral ministry. That wasn't my goal, mind you. I loved Christ, and I was committed to the Scriptures. I was just mistaken regarding what the Bible required of me. I considered my eagerness to separate—even from others who believed, taught, and tried to obey Scripture—to be a virtue.

Here's my theory on why I've changed a bit in recent years, along with a whole host of ministry friends. We didn't know the Scriptures well when we were wide-eyed twenty-year-olds. As a result, we swallowed everything we were fed—and the vast majority of what we were taught was great! But we hadn't yet developed the ability to discern, to swallow the meat and spit out the bones. However, after ten or fifteen years of preaching multiple times a week, we came to know the Scriptures really well. We learned discernment. And occasionally, we learned that we needed to adjust some of the lessons we had been taught years before.[39]

That's my story. And it's not a sad one. I'm not remotely bitter. I just had to grow up, and I believe I did. To try to help others going through that

---

39 It is inaccurate and ungracious to assume that all changes of opinion reflect sinful compromise. Sometimes altering one's position on an issue is a matter of maturity, not mutiny. Remember, the Bereans were considered noble for comparing what they had been taught with the Scriptures (Acts 17:11). The Christian's goal isn't to toe the party line, but rather to align with the Word of God. It is a good thing to carefully investigate what the Bible teaches. We need not fear it.

same process, I've boiled down the spiritual lessons that helped me turn from my divisive spirit to six "prescriptions"—six antidotes to schism. The medicines that delivered me from self-righteous schism are the gospel, grace, the Great Commission, the sufficiency of Scripture, humility, and courage.

Antidote 1: The Gospel

Books about the gospel have multiplied in the last twenty years or so. I love that. But familiarity may breed contempt: "Oh, *the gospel* changed your thinking on sinful separation. Yawn." Perhaps it sounds cliché, but it's true. Here's the reality of my experience in pastoral ministry: The more passionate I became about the centrality of the gospel, the less I felt the need to fight over less important issues.

The gospel matters most. That's not just my opinion. Paul writes in 1 Corinthians 15:3 that the gospel is "of first importance." All Scripture is inspired and profitable (2 Timothy 3:16), but not all Scripture bears equal doctrinal weight. Paul clearly teaches doctrinal triage—the idea that some doctrines are more crucial than others (as we'll discuss in chapter 13).

Now, I'm not suggesting that pastors should preach only evangelistic messages on the cross week after week. We are responsible to preach "the whole counsel of God" (Acts 20:27)—a command that I believe is best obeyed by preaching expository messages through entire books of the Bible. But preaching through the New Testament *is* preaching the gospel—its meaning and significance, its implications and obligations, and its life-changing power. The gospel isn't just the milk of the Word; it's also the meat! It's the entirety of the New Testament, properly understood. See Romans, or Ephesians, or Hebrews. Christians never graduate beyond the gospel; we just grow in our understanding of its infinite depths.

When the gospel began to truly enthrall me, minutiae like whether a Christian had a tattoo or how they dressed for church just stopped mattering. Zambian pastor Conrad Mbewe writes, "If we keep our eyes on Christ and his work on the cross for us, there will be less cause for the levels of disunity that have plagued the church across history all the way to our present day."[40] Focusing on the gospel dissolves petty disputes. If you have schismatic tendencies, study the gospel more intentionally.[41]

Antidote 2: Grace

The second antidote to schism is related to the first. The true gospel is a gospel of *grace*. My distinction here is this: The gospel is an *objective fact*—Christianity rests on historical events that include the death, burial, and resurrection of Jesus Christ. But I'm thinking of grace here as a *subjective experience* in addition to an absolute truth. Yes, we are saved by grace. That truth, thankfully, I never doubted. But we also *grow* in grace (2 Peter 3:18). We *stand* in grace (Romans 5:2). We *endure trials* by grace (2 Corinthians 12:7–10). Paul's common New Testament blessing, "Grace to you," wasn't just a "holy hello." It was a prayer, as well as a constant reminder of the Christian's dependence on God's grace for every facet of life. As I've written elsewhere, "Rightly understood and applied, God's grace is your spiritual oxygen…your lifeline…your only reliable coping mechanism."[42]

While I never bought into legalism as a means of justification, I did unwittingly embrace legalism as a means to sanctification. You are saved by grace, I would preach—but then it's time to *work*. Follow these rules. Avoid these activities (even if Scripture doesn't explicitly forbid them). Cultivate these habits (even if Scripture doesn't explicitly command them). I was wrong.

While I acknowledge that growth in Christlikeness is indeed synergistic (I work *out* as God works *in*, Philippians 2:12–13), my emphasis at the time was on Christian performance—a barely veiled behaviorism. To be clear, my desire to obey Scripture and my cultivation of godly habits toward that end was good; my tendency to *depend* on those efforts was not.

I thought I was promoting Spirit-enabled discipleship. But…

I promoted the kind of asceticism Scripture forbids. I sincerely believed that abiding by a list of extrabiblical rules would help people grow as Chris-

---

40   Conrad Mbewe, *Unity: Striving Side by Side for the Gospel* (Wheaton, IL: Crossway, 2024), 31.

41   Some of my favorite books on the gospel include Jerry Bridges' book *The Gospel for Real Life*, Michael Barrett's book *Complete in Him*, and John Stott's book *The Cross of Christ*. "Take up and read."

42   Chris Anderson, "Grace to You, Mom!" in *Gospel Meditations for Mothers* (Church Works Media, 2018), Day 1.

tians. But I ignored the fact that Scripture specifically repudiates seemingly pious asceticism:

> If with Christ you died to the elemental spirits of the world, why, as if you were still alive in the world, do you submit to regulations—"Do not handle, Do not taste, Do not touch" (referring to things that all perish as they are used)—according to human precepts and teachings? These have indeed an appearance of wisdom in promoting self-made religion and asceticism and severity to the body, but they are of no value in stopping the indulgence of the flesh. (Colossians 2:20–23)

> Now the Spirit expressly says that in later times some will depart from the faith by devoting themselves to deceitful spirits and teachings of demons, through the insincerity of liars whose consciences are seared, who forbid marriage and require abstinence from foods that God created to be received with thanksgiving by those who believe and know the truth. For everything created by God is good, and nothing is to be rejected if it is received with thanksgiving, for it is made holy by the word of God and prayer. (1 Timothy 4:1–5)

I embraced the kind of judgmentalism Scripture forbids. I was like the Pharisee in Luke 18:9–14 in that I thanked God that I wasn't like the compromising Christians all around me who used drums and drank wine. I was more than willing to judge fellow believers who loved Jesus but differed from me on nonessentials. I needed this reproof from Puritan Thomas Brooks: "It is sad to consider that saints should have many eyes to behold one another's infirmities, and not one eye to see each other's graces."[43]

I elevated my convictions in a way that Scripture forbids. Whereas Matthew 15:9 condemns the Pharisees for elevating "the commandments of men" to the level of Scripture, I was content to impose my extrabiblical preferences on others. I was exacting. I truly believed that if I could see a person's CD collection (young people, think "playlist") I could tell you whether or not she loved Jesus. If your church didn't have a Sunday night service, your commitment was suspect. If a guy had long hair or an earring, he was worldly, even effeminate. If you danced at a wedding, you were sensual. If you exceeded the speed limit—seriously, I preached

---

43   Thomas Brooks, *Precious Remedies Against Satan's Devices* in *The Works of Thomas Brooks*, ed. Alexander B. Grosart (Carlisle, PA: The Banner of Truth Trust, 2001), 1:128.

this!—you were an egregious lawbreaker. My focus was on externals, and it was graceless.

I strained at spiritual gnats while swallowing spiritual camels in a way that Scripture forbids. I emphasized minutiae while neglecting what Jesus calls "the weightier matters of the law" like "justice, mercy, and faithfulness" (Matthew 23:23). So, in my way of thinking then, the music you listened to mattered as much as or more than how you treated your wife and kids. How you dressed for church mattered more than your relationships with your lost neighbors. In almost every decision, conservatism trumped compassion.

Tragically, I wasn't the only one. It's been disheartening over the years to hear of church leaders who emphasized spiritual gnats like excessively modest dress and the avoidance of movie theaters but who were simultaneously swallowing spiritual camels like the slander of faithful Christians or the sexual assault of minors. Sexual abuse has been a scandal in the church and a life-altering tragedy for the victims. Jesus' verdict in such cases is unambiguous (Matthew 18:5–6). I don't think it is only my perception that cases of sexual abuse (and sometimes, resulting cover-ups) have become more prevalent among extremely conservative ministries and families. At times it has felt like those obsessing about *very* detailed Christian standards are overcompensating—like a driver who carefully obeys traffic laws because he has a body in the trunk of his car. This is not grace.

Grace is my favorite English word. Recognizing that grace is the key to the entire Christian experience—not just the beginning of the Christian experience—is life-changing. When you embrace grace, you'll be less focused on minor issues and more deferential to faithful Christian brothers and sisters. As English pastor D. Martin Lloyd-Jones writes, "The Christian life starts with grace, it must continue with grace, it ends with grace."[44]

As I have grown in grace myself, I have made it a point of emphasis in my teaching. I thank the Lord for His help in encouraging Christians to develop a "culture of grace" in their churches, which I have defined in this way: *When every Christian is more aware of his own sins than of others', and more focused on Christ than either.*

---

44   Iain H. Murray, *D. Martyn Lloyd-Jones: Letters 1919–1981* (Carlisle, PA: The Banner of Truth Trust, 1994), 237.

To those who, like me, are recovering from well-meaning legalism, I pray that you'll come to appreciate and experience God's transforming and liberating grace.

Grace to You

To hearts that sink in shame
When sin again has stirred,
To those who drown in blame
The gospel has a word:
"Grace to you. Grace to you."

To all who long to grow,
But hate the things they do,
To those whose hope is low,
The Savior speaks to you:
"Grace to you. Grace to you."

To those who bear a thorn
Which God has not removed,
To all the ones who mourn,
The Father brings good news:
"Grace to you. Grace to you."

Chorus

Grace that seeks, grace that keeps,
Grace sufficient to sustain the one who weeps,
Grace to break your sin's embrace,
God's relentless, boundless, endless amazing grace.[45]

Antidote 3: The Great Commission

Jesus' words in John 4:32 move me. The disciples had just returned from a Samaritan village, and they found Him evangelizing a Samaritan woman by an ancient well. *Weird,* they thought, though they said nothing out loud. When she walked away—*finally!*—they offered Jesus some lunch. Notice His response: "I have food to eat that you do not know about." They missed the point, wondering if someone had fed Jesus while they were away. But

---

45   "Grace to You" is a new hymn by Chris Anderson (lyrics) and Heather Schopf (music). ©2024 Forever Be Sure. All rights reserved. Used by permission. Download a free hymn version: churchworksmedia.com/product/grace-to-you-free. Download a vocal arrangement: foreverbesure.com/product/grace-to-you.

Jesus repeated and explained Himself: "My food is to do the will of him who sent me and to accomplish his work" (John 4:34).

Jesus was telling the disciples that He was *hungry for souls*. The work the Father had sent Him to do was to collect worshipers (John 4:23)—to "seek and save the lost" (Luke 19:10). *When a sinner is coming to Christ, who cares about lunch?!* Well, the disciples did. And often, we do.

The Great Commission is supposed to consume our attention. We're supposed to be voraciously hungry to see the lost won to Christ. But instead, we're distracted, sometimes by worldliness and sometimes by intramural skirmishes with fellow Christians. Either way, our neglect of souls is scandalous.

Leaning into the Great Commission is an essential antidote to overcoming a schismatic spirit. In my roles as a pastor and a missions catalyst, I've spoken with scores of missionaries who marvel that the American church is so distracted by "first-world problems." Only in the pampered West do we have the luxury to waste time debating issues like whether it's appropriate to wear jeans to church instead of matters of eternal consequence. Actually, we *don't* have that luxury. We're in a war for souls, and we dare not waste time on pointless debates.

Members of the U.S. Armed Forces may fight among themselves when they're safely tucked away on American soil. Marine "jarheads" and Navy "squids" can scuffle in San Diego. But when they're on the front lines battling a real enemy, marines, pilots, soldiers, and sailors see each other as allies, not adversaries. Their lives and the success of their mission depend on working together.

Were we more aware that we *are* on the frontlines in reaching the lost, we'd fight one another less. I'm sure of that. If you're trying to grow out of your schismatic spirit, read a missionary biography. Write a missionary an email. Pray for the missionaries your church supports. Pray for more laborers, as commanded in Matthew 9:38. Get out of America and onto a mission field, even if it's just for a few weeks. See if the work doesn't take your mind off of Bible versions, worship wars, and dress standards for a bit.

We need to stay on mission. As my friend Jim Berg puts it, if we're only "holding the fort" and not "storming the gates" through Great Commission ministry, we need to repent.

Antidote 4: Sola Scriptura

The fourth medicine to fight your schismatic spirit is the doctrine of the sufficiency of Scripture. This should be an easy one for every lover of the Bible. We're committed not only to the inspiration, inerrancy, and authority of Scripture—all of which conservative Roman Catholics could affirm, by the way—but also to the *sufficiency* of Scripture. The doctrinal statements of the churches I've pastored use language like this: "We believe that the Bible is our only rule of faith and practice."

Traditionally, that teaching has been referred to as *sola scriptura*—the first of the five *solas* of the Protestant Reformation.[46] Protestants don't believe in Jesus-plus, faith-plus, or grace-plus. We believe that we are saved by grace alone through faith alone in Christ alone for God's glory alone. And all of that right doctrine grows out of the Scriptures—*alone*.

Bob Kauflin and I wrote about the doctrine of *sola scriptura* in our 2017 song "Reformation Hymn," written in honor of the five-hundredth anniversary of the Protestant Reformation. This is what we believe, celebrate, and sing about:

> We will trust God's Word alone,
> Where His perfect will is known;
> Our traditions shift like sand
> While His Truth forever stands.[47]

Human traditions are sand. Human opinions are sand. Human rules are sand. Scripture alone is the rock—the unshakable and authoritative foundation. The entirety of the Christian faith rests on this truth.

That's why Protestants call the doctrine of *sola scriptura* "the formal principle" of the Reformation. It's the starting point. It's the linchpin. It's this doctrine that was the basis for the rest of the *solas*. The doctrine of the sufficiency of Scripture is not one we can surrender, even unintentionally, without drastic consequences.

---

46   See my article "The Greatest of These" in *Gospel Meditations on the Reformation* (Church Works Media, 2016), Day 19.

47   Lyrics from "Reformation Hymn" by Chris Anderson and Bob Kauflin. ©2017 Sovereign Grace Praise (BMI), Church Works Worship (ASCAP) (adm at IntegratedRights.com). All rights reserved. Used by permission. Download a free hymn version: churchworksmedia.com/product/reformation-hymn-free.

Because of this belief that Scripture is the foundation of our faith, we would be horrified if someone were to stand in the pulpit and rip out pages of the Bible. But we should be equally horrified when someone stands in the pulpit and *adds to* Scripture. The doctrine of Scripture's sufficiency precludes our supplementing the Bible, whether the addition is a Papal Bull, the Koran, the Book of Mormon, or (and here's the critical point for our discussion of schism) *insistence on our personal preferences*. Revelation 22:19 forbids removing portions of the Bible. But Revelation 22:18 forbids *adding to* Scripture—which is the greater temptation for modern Christians. God's Word is complete and perfect. As 1 Corinthians 4:6 insists, we must not "go beyond what is written." The canon is closed. Scripture is sufficient.[48]

R. B. Kuiper riffs on the pseudo-pious way in which Christians divide over extrabiblical issues—things they've *added* to what God states in Scripture:

> Protestant churches have been split by the demand of serious-minded Christians that church members live by eleven or twelve commandments instead of ten. It is at this point that the virtue of piety degenerates into the vice of piosity. At the same point the sin of sectarianism has frequently raised its ugly head. To divide the church on what according to the word of God is an "indifferent" matter—that is to say, a practice that God has neither condemned nor commanded—is the essence of sectarianism. Once more, failure to keep the various teachings of Scripture in balance with each other and the consequent stressing of one or some of them out of all proportion to others, have frequently destroyed the visible unity of Christ's church. Riding a theological hobby is by no means an innocent pastime. Of such sins it behooves churches everywhere to repent, and from them they must desist.[49]

There is an "inner Pharisee" in each of us. We are all tempted to elevate our personal convictions and standards to the level of Scripture—practically, if not formally. Christ's verdict on the Pharisees' habit of adding to the Word

---

48   Jamieson, Fausset, and Brown write, "Revere the silence of Holy Writ, as much as its declarations: so you will less dogmatize on what is not expressly revealed (Deuteronomy 29:29)." Robert Jamieson, A. R. Fausset, and David Brown, *A Commentary Critical and Explanatory on the Old and New Testaments* (Grand Rapids, MI: Zondervan Publishing House, 1999), 2:270. Emphasis in original.

49   R. B. Kuiper, *The Glorious Body of Christ: A Scriptural Appreciation of the One Holy Church* (Edinburgh: Banner of Truth, 1967), 53–54.

of God is one we should heed. Quoting Isaiah 29:13, Jesus concludes, "This people honors me with their lips, but their heart is far from me; in vain do they worship me, teaching as doctrines the commandments of men" (Matthew 15:8–9). Treating our extrabiblical preferences as though they were biblical doctrine reveals hearts that are far from God. That's sobering.

I loved my time at Bob Jones University. It wasn't a perfect place, but I grew tremendously during the seven years I studied there. Thanks to the training I received, I was well-equipped for ministry. I'm grateful enough that three of my four daughters (and virtually all my money!) went there as well.

The single best thing I learned at BJU was the absolute authority of Scripture. My professors hammered that into me, and I'm grateful for it. But here's the thing: I learned that lesson *so well* that some of the other lessons I was taught by fundamentalists over the years can't get through that filter. My commitment to the exclusive authority of Scripture has led me to adjust my opinions on issues like worship, entertainment, and excessive separation.

We must renew our commitment to the authority—and *sufficiency*—of Scripture.

Antidote 5: Humility

Perhaps the besetting sin that led me to unnecessary divisions from faithful brothers and sisters in Christ was my own pride. I wouldn't be the first. Solomon informs us, "Only by pride cometh contention" (Proverbs 13:10 KJV). James 4:1–3 says that quarreling and infighting are caused by our selfish desires. My eagerness to critique other Christians wreaked of arrogance.

So how did I conquer my pride? (Just *typing* that sentence made me laugh at myself.) Of course, I *haven't* conquered my pride. I can't even pretend to be humble. I'll be battling my own sense of self-importance until heaven. But I have adjusted my self-identity. The more I studied the gospel (antidote 1), the more I conceived of myself as a sinner saved by grace (antidote 2), not a really obedient Christian whom God was lucky to have on His side. It wasn't self-loathing (which can be a squirrelly form of self-loving). It was just acknowledging the objective fact which Paul relates in 1 Timothy 1:15: "I'm the biggest sinner I know."

Tim Keller's little book *The Prodigal God* helped me discern my own schismatic arrogance. The book takes a fresh look at Luke 15. The real bad guy in the parable of the prodigal son wasn't the prodigal but his legalistic older brother, whom Jesus used to expose the self-righteousness of the scribes and Pharisees. They had openly groused that "this man [Jesus] receives sinners" (vv. 1–2). And so, He went after them, revealing their arrogance and lostness through three successive parables. The parables of the lost sheep (vv. 3–7), the lost coin (vv. 8–10), and the lost son (vv. 11–32) all contrast the Father's love for repentant sinners with the scribes' and Pharisees' disdain for sinners. The younger brother was just an extra; the older brother was the leading character—and the worse of the two rebels.

Keller's book was convicting. I saw myself in the older brother—in his judgmentalism, his pride, and his self-righteous belief that the Father *owed* him something for his good behavior. I was exposed. It stung, but it was helpful.

More than that, I was challenged by the meekness of Christ (Matthew 11:29; 12:20). I was struck by the gentleness required of pastors (see the qualifications in 1 Timothy 3:1–7; 2 Timothy 2:24–25; and Titus 1:5–9) and by the beautiful virtues produced by the Spirit (Galatians 5:22–23). I was impressed by the humility of Peter in 1 Peter 5:1–5—a very different Peter from the braggart who constantly jockeyed for position in the four Gospels (Luke 9:46; 22:24, 33). And I was rebuked by this good word from J. C. Ryle's classic book *Holiness*: "There is no surer mark of backsliding and falling off in grace than an increasing disposition to find fault, pick holes, and see weak points in others."[50]

That was me. As a schismatic legalist, I needed a good dose of Spirit-produced humility. And I still do.

Antidote 6: Courage

A final medicine that has helped me turn from unbiblical schism is good old-fashioned courage. As I have repented of my sinful pride and divisiveness, I've made an important commitment: I determine to make ministry and life decisions on the basis of Scripture, as I understand it—not the opinions of others. It was a decision that relieved my conscience and strengthened my character. But it has come at a cost. I have had to be

---

50   Ryle, *Holiness*, 87.

willing to be a villain in the minds of some, if necessary, in order to align myself with Scripture. And trust me, that can sting.

Adjusting my practice of biblical separation has cost me some friendships. It has also cost me some opportunities. Ironically, having carried out spurious separation for years, I've now been on the *receiving* side of it—I've been separated *from*. Speaking gigs have been rescinded. Doors have closed. Angry emails have hit my inbox. And it's okay.

The Lord Jesus commanded us not to call men "father," nor be called "master" (Matthew 23:9–10). John Owen takes this as a command to free yourself "from the bondage of subjection to the dictates of men (and the innumerable evils, with endless entanglements, thence ensuing)."[51] Owen's point is that it is dangerous for the Christian to submit his conscience to any person or institution outside of God Himself. Sure, there's a place to limit legitimate liberties for the sake of ministry (1 Corinthians 8:13; 9:1–15, 22). But cowardice—the willingness to "go along to get along"—is a constant threat to true spirituality.

I joke that my life verse is Proverbs 29:25: "The fear of man lays a snare, but whoever trusts in the LORD is safe." I'm human, so I don't like to make people angry. I like to be liked. But the fear of man is a *trap*. Fear is debilitating. And fear is the opposite of faith. Proverbs 28:1 strikes the same note, telling us that "the righteous are bold as a lion." There's a worthy life goal—to be bold as a lion on matters of biblical obedience! John MacArthur writes, "Cowardice and authentic faith are antithetical."[52]

But be warned: Living out Proverbs 29:25 may invite criticism. Buckle up, buttercup—there may be turbulence ahead. And God will give you the grace to endure it. How? First—back to antidotes 4 and 5: Cling to the Word as your sufficient guide, and remain humble and teachable. But recognize that true humility will sometimes require you to bear the consequences of unpopular but principled decisions. Determine to endure disapproval, by God's grace. Prize the ability to look yourself in the mirror with a clear conscience. And remember Paul's charge from Galatians 1:10: "For am I now seeking the approval of man, or of God? Or am I trying to

---

51   John Owen, *The Works of John Owen*, ed. William H. Gould (Carlisle, PA: The Banner of Truth Trust, 1967), 13:92.

52   John MacArthur, *The Truth War: Fighting for Certainty in an Age of Deception* (Nashville, TN: Thomas Nelson, 2007), xv.

please man? If I were still trying to please man, I would not be a servant of Christ."

Making decisions regarding fellowship and separation on the basis of biblical fidelity rather than the opinions of my alma mater, my ministry friends, or potential critics has been sanctifying for me, and it's been productive for ministry. And so I've enjoyed partnering with many friends from fundamentalist backgrounds over the years. These are my people.

But I've also enjoyed working alongside conservative evangelicals in recent years. They share my love for the truth, though they may not share or even understand my background. Still, if we agree on and defend core Bible doctrine together, *these are my people, too.*

One of my favorite examples of how similar those two worlds are comes from a conference I helped to host in Atlanta in 2017 to celebrate the five-hundredth anniversary of the Reformation. I invited an esteemed church history professor from Bob Jones University, the late Dr. Ed Panosian, to do five dramatic, in-character presentations of several Protestant Reformers. And I invited Phil Johnson from Grace to You to preach on Reformation doctrines. Apparently, Dr. Panosian didn't comprehend that he would be sharing the platform with Phil, and it caused him quite a bit of anxiety, as he wasn't sure how BJU would view the varied his sharing the platform with someone from outside of the fundamentalist sphere. I remember the voicemail I first received from Dr. Panosian, in his inimitably rich voice: "Chris, I look forward to the conference. But *who* or *what* is Phil Johnson?!"

Dr. Panosian eventually got a green light from his former employer to attend and speak at the conference. As a retired professor, he didn't really need it, but his temporary trepidation sheds some light on the culture of fundamentalism during his lifetime. I'll never forget sitting next to him on the front row of the auditorium during Phil Johnson's first sermon that day—a no-nonsense exegetical masterpiece. When Phil concluded, Dr. Panosian turned to me, mouth agape and eyebrows raised, and exclaimed, "That was *excellent!*" My response to him was a big smile and one word: "*Right?*" Phil similarly enjoyed Dr. Panosian's presentations, and he eventually endorsed my book about the great man.[53]

---

53   One of the highlights of my literary life was the writing of Dr. Panosian's biography as a result of the time we shared during that conference. By God's grace, we captured his remarkable story just a

We're not so different, and actually meeting those on the other side of our arbitrary lines can sometimes clear up our misperceptions.

Personally, I've labored hard to prove this point in my own ministry work. Hosting guests from outside narrower fundamentalist circles—like John MacArthur, Al Mohler, Voddie Baucham, and Steve Green—at the church I pastored in Atlanta was a blessing. Recording an album with Stonebriar Community Church was a delight. Working with leaders like Carl Trueman, Bob Kauflin, and Conrad Mbewe on Church Works Media projects—and receiving kind endorsements by scores of other leaders over the years—has highlighted our like-mindedness in an instructive way.

Similarly, recording an album in 2023 with a fresh sound and more emotional expressiveness than some deem acceptable was worth the pushback. Even writing this book is worth the criticism it may invite. Each of these decisions was made with an open Bible and a clear conscience. And as best as I know how, I'm living by *principle*, not fear.

Not everybody will draw the lines where I have. That's fine. But I'm begging you: Determine your fellowship decisions on the basis of Scripture, not your friends or critics. Proverbs commands us not to negotiate with terrorists. (Okay, I made that up.) But seriously, if you begin making your decisions based on someone else's conscience, you'll never stop. You'll be stuck there. I'm not telling you to intentionally tick people off. But don't live in fear, either. Pray, take courage, and obey the Scriptures as you see fit. Say with Luther-like conviction: "Here I stand."

---

short time before he went to his reward. Check out *Panosian: A Story of God's Gracious Providence* (Church Works Media, 2018)—available in print, digital, and audio formats.

◄ PART 2 ►

WHEN SEPARATION IS ESSENTIAL

"These two things, truth and love, Jesus asks for His own as of vital moment: truth as the badge of distinction between His Church and the world; love as the bond which unites believers of the truth into a holy brotherhood of witness-bearers to the truth. These two things the Church should ever keep in view as of co-ordinate importance: not sacrificing love to truth, dividing those who should be one by insisting on too minute and detailed a testimony; nor sacrificing truth to love, making the Church a very broad, comprehensive society, but a society without a vocation or *raison d'être*, having no truth to guard and teach, or testimony to bear."

—*A. B. Bruce*[54]

---

54   A. B. Bruce, *The Training of the Twelve* (Grand Rapids, MI: Kregel Publications, 1988), 457.

CHAPTER 5

SCRIPTURE COMMANDS SEPARATION FROM FALSE TEACHERS

"Do not be unequally yoked with unbelievers. For what partnership has righteousness with lawlessness? Or what fellowship has light with darkness?"

—2 Corinthians 6:17

Perhaps you feel a tension as you read this book. You might wonder, *Is Chris calling for unity or separation? For peace or fighting?* The answer is yes—both—because Scripture calls for both. Not all separation is sinful. Indeed, faithfulness to the Scriptures requires separation. While I repudiate unbiblical schism, I am a biblical separatist. You should be too. And that deserves explanation.

As always, we must begin with the biblical data. What does Scripture say about separation from apostasy and apostates? Much.

The Biblical Record

It may come as a surprise to many readers to learn that every book of the New Testament includes a warning against false teachers! (Every book but Philemon, that is—a little book that addresses a personal issue and was sent alongside the book of Colossians, which spends four chapters battling false teaching.) Books devoted almost entirely to false teaching include Galatians, 2 Peter, 2 John, and Jude. But the entire New Testament calls for absolute intolerance of false teaching. Here's an inexhaustive but compelling sample:

Beware of false prophets, who come to you in sheep's clothing but inwardly are ravenous wolves. (Matthew 7:15)

Jesus said to [his disciples], "Watch and beware of the leaven of the Pharisees and Sadducees".... Then they understood that he did not tell them to beware of the leaven of bread, but of the teaching of the Pharisees and Sadducees. (Matthew 16:6, 12)

I know that after my departure fierce wolves will come in among you, not sparing the flock; and from among your own selves will arise men speaking twisted things, to draw away the disciples after them. Therefore, be alert, remembering that for three years I did not cease night or day to admonish every one with tears. (Acts 20:29–31)

Do not be unequally yoked with unbelievers. For what partnership has righteousness with lawlessness? Or what fellowship has light with darkness? What accord has Christ with Belial? Or what portion does a believer share with an unbeliever? What agreement has the temple of God with idols? For we are the temple of the living God; as God said, "I will make my dwelling among them and walk among them, and I will be their God, and they shall be my people. Therefore go out from their midst, and be separate from them, says the Lord, and touch no unclean thing; then I will welcome you, and I will be a father to you, and you shall be sons and daughters to me, says the Lord Almighty." (2 Corinthians 6:14–18)

Such men are false apostles, deceitful workmen, disguising themselves as apostles of Christ. (2 Corinthians 11:13)

I am astonished that you are so quickly deserting him who called you in the grace of Christ and are turning to a different gospel—not that there is another one, but there are some who trouble you and want to distort the gospel of Christ. But even if we or an angel from heaven should preach to you a gospel contrary to the one we preached to you, let him be accursed. As we have said before, so now I say again: If anyone is preaching to you a gospel contrary to the one you received, let him be accursed. (Galatians 1:6–9)

If anyone teaches a different doctrine and does not agree with the sound words of our Lord Jesus Christ and the teaching that accords with godliness, he is puffed up with conceit and understands nothing.

He has an unhealthy craving for controversy and for quarrels about words, which produce envy, dissension, slander, evil suspicions, and constant friction among people who are depraved in mind and deprived of the truth, imagining that godliness is a means of gain. (1 Timothy 6:3–5)

But false prophets also arose among the people, just as there will be false teachers among you, who will secretly bring in destructive heresies, even denying the Master who bought them, bringing upon themselves swift destruction. (2 Peter 2:1)

Beloved, do not believe every spirit, but test the spirits to see whether they are from God, for many false prophets have gone out into the world. (1 John 4:1)

If anyone comes to you and does not bring this teaching, do not receive him into your house or give him any greeting, for whoever greets him takes part in his wicked works. (2 John 10–11)

Beloved, although I was very eager to write to you about our common salvation, I found it necessary to write appealing to you to contend for the faith that was once for all delivered to the saints. For certain people have crept in unnoticed who long ago were designated for this condemnation, ungodly people, who pervert the grace of our God into sensuality and deny our only Master and Lord, Jesus Christ. (Jude 3–4)

"I know your works, your toil and your patient endurance, and how you cannot bear with those who are evil, but have tested those who call themselves apostles and are not, and found them to be false." (Revelation 2:2; contrast this with those who tolerate false teachers in Revelation 2:14–16, 20–23)

Scripture clearly and repeatedly calls for separation from false teachers. That means that partnering with unbelievers in ecumenical religious efforts is wrong, even when the goal is evangelism. It means that believers in countries where the gospel is mixed with tribal religion in a strange syncretism need to identify that error and call people to "turn to God from idols" (1 Thessalonians 1:9). It means that we cannot cooperate in spiritual endeavors with unbelievers—whether Roman Catholics, theological liberals, or universalists. *Biblical orthodoxy is a boundary to biblical fellow-*

ship. To miss or ignore these warnings is a willful dereliction of duty—one that confuses the very gospel.

Has the doctrine of separation sometimes been misapplied? Certainly. I've lived it. But abuse of the truth doesn't excuse abandonment of the truth. Scripture calls for Christians to separate from false teaching and false teachers. Where there is no doctrinal purity there can be no spiritual unity.[55]

Pastor Conrad Mbewe hits the nail on the head:

> The fact that Christian unity is secured in Christ and applied by the Holy Spirit means that only true Christians, who have responded to the gospel in genuine repentance and faith, should be embraced in this unity. This means that the gospel should be the dividing line for this unity. Where there is a seriously defective understanding of the gospel, we cannot with good conscience forge unity. That would betray the Christian faith altogether. Some churches are "synagogues of Satan" (Rev. 3:9). We must not be seen holding hands with them. They are more of a mission field than mission partners....
>
> Those who believe in salvation by grace alone, through faith alone, and in Christ alone cannot serve together in gospel endeavors with those who think that our good works merit God's favor in salvation. The two messages are diametrical opposites.[56]

Charles Spurgeon and Billy Graham

Let me illustrate the need to separate from apostasy by contrasting two beloved and influential Christian leaders—one who practiced biblical separation and one who did not: Charles Spurgeon and Billy Graham.

Charles Spurgeon was one of the most influential gospel preachers the English language has ever known. His love for souls was unbounded, and his eloquence is still unsurpassed. Spurgeon had a worldwide reach in his own day, and it continues well over a century after his death. And yet, Spurgeon conscientiously refused to cooperate with those who denied

---

55   Wayne Grudem makes a compelling case for separation for the sake of doctrinal purity in "When, Why, and for What Should We Draw New Boundaries?" in *Beyond the Bounds: Open Theism and the Undermining of Biblical Christianity*, ed. John Piper, Justin Taylor, and Paul Kjoss Helseth (Wheaton, IL: Crossway, 2003), 339–70.

56   Mbewe, 54, 80.

biblical doctrine—so much so, in fact, that he himself was ostracized and censured by his brothers (and his brother!) in the famous "downgrade controversy" that troubled the Baptist Union in England during his final years. Though he was in a distinct minority regarding separation, Spurgeon repeatedly sounded the alarm against false teachers and those who tolerated them:

> Believers in Christ's atonement are now in declared union with those who make light of it; believers in Holy Scripture are in confederacy with those who deny plenary inspiration; those who hold evangelical doctrine are in open alliance with those who call the fall a fable, who deny the personality of the Holy Ghost, who call justification by faith immoral, and hold that there is another probation after death.... Complicity with error will take from the best of men the power to enter any successful protest against it.... It is our solemn conviction that there should be no pretense of fellowship. Fellowship with known and vital error is participation in sin.[57]

That fiery excerpt comes from Spurgeon's publication, *The Sword and the Trowel*. The very title of the monthly magazine acknowledged (with a nod to Nehemiah 4) that Christians are *always* defending and *always* building. Wielding two trowels is dangerous, as is wielding two swords. Spurgeon wrote about the publication's purpose in its first issue: "We would ply the Trowel with untiring hand for the building up of Jerusalem's dilapidated walls, and wield the Sword with vigour and valour against the enemies of the Truth."[58]

Listen to Spurgeon as he again describes the necessity of courageously defending the truth:

> The Church of Christ is continually represented under the figure of an army; yet its Captain is the Prince of Peace; its object is the establishment of peace, and its soldiers are men of a peaceful disposition. The spirit of war is at the extremely opposite point to the spirit of the gospel.

---

57 C. H. Spurgeon, *The Sword and the Trowel*, November 1887.

58 C. H. Spurgeon, *The Sword and the Trowel*, January 1865.

Yet nevertheless, the church on earth has [been], and until the second advent must be, the church militant, the church armed, the church warring, the church conquering. And how is this?

It is in the very order of things that so it must be. Truth could not be in this world if it were not a warring thing, and we should at once suspect that it were not true if error were friends with it. The spotless purity of truth must always be at war with the blackness of heresy and lies.[59]

An unfortunate contrast to Spurgeon's separatism was Billy Graham's inclusivism. The beloved gospel preacher did a *great deal* of good. I've experienced this personally, not merely as a student of twentieth-century church history. My grandfather was led to Christ in part through attending a Graham evangelistic crusade in Los Angeles in 1974.

But Graham made a conscious decision during his New York City campaign of 1957 that he could reach more people with the truth if he collaborated with a wide spectrum of churches and church leaders—including known theological liberals and Roman Catholics.[60] "Graham forces," writes historian George Marsden, "were raising a chorus against separatism."[61] Graham preached the gospel with wonderful power, and I rejoice in it (Philippians 1:18). The statistics reported at the campaign's conclusion were astounding: There were 53,626 professions of faith, 22,000 of which came from people aged twenty-one and younger.[62]

But Graham's alignment with those who denied the gospel and his practice of sending new converts to liberal churches did a great deal of harm. A Graham-authorized book on the New York City campaign of 1957 recorded Graham's inclusive policies in his own words: "Let me make this very clear. I intend to go anywhere, any time, and be sponsored by anybody, if by so doing I can preach the Gospel of Jesus Christ." He later added, "People don't like our policy of sending converts back to the churches of their choice."[63] Christian historian Iain Murray lays the blame

59   Charles Spurgeon, *The Metropolitan Tabernacle Pulpit* (London: Passmore & Alabaster, 1879), 5:41.

60   McCune, *Promise*, 45.

61   Marsden, *Reforming*, 189.

62   Curtis Mitchell, *God in the Garden: The Story of the Billy Graham New York Crusade* (Garden City, NY: Doubleday & Company, Inc., 1957), 177.

63   Ibid., 107. See Marsden, *Reforming*, 162.

for an "Evangelicalism Divided" at the feet of Graham and his ecumenical supporters.[64] Graham did so much good, but his record is a mixed bag due to his refusal to obey Scripture's commands to separate from unbelief.

Tragically, Graham's inclusive practices eventually eroded his doctrine—or at least led to shockingly imprudent comments. For example, upon receiving an honorary doctorate from Belmont Abbey College (a Roman Catholic institution), Graham gushed that it was time for Protestants and Catholics to "greet each other as brothers." He went on to preach that he and his Catholic hosts believed the same gospel.[65] Still worse, Graham seemed to indicate during an interview at Robert Schuller's Crystal Cathedral that those who have never heard of Jesus—including Muslims, Buddhists, and atheists—but have done their best, are part of the body of Christ and will be with us in heaven.[66] Behavior eventually affects belief, even for the world's greatest evangelist.

It gives me no pleasure to highlight Graham's errors. Would that we had more believers who were so burdened for the lost and so effective in communicating the gospel! But we must not disobey Scripture or minimize heresy, even for the sake of evangelism.

Jude's Command to "Contend"

Let me make two points of clarification regarding separation, both from the example of Jude in his short biblical letter. First, we should be enthralled with the gospel, not with the battle. Jude was a reluctant warrior.

> Beloved, although I was very eager to write to you about our common salvation, I found it necessary to write appealing to you to contend for the faith that was once for all delivered to the saints. (Jude 3)

---

64   Iain Murray, *Evangelicalism Divided: A Record of the Crucial Change in the Years 1950 to 2000* (Carlisle, PA: The Banner of Truth Trust, 2000), 24–50. Murray writes, "The developing [Billy Graham Evangelistic Association] ministry has been accompanied by a disastrous weakening of evangelical belief." Ibid., 72. Murray's pastor, D. Martin Lloyd-Jones, similarly blamed those who wandered from orthodox doctrine for disrupting evangelical unity—*not* the conscientious brothers who, like himself, refused to tolerate their apostasy. D. Martin Lloyd-Jones, "Evangelical Unity." mljtrust.org/sermons/itinerant-preaching/evangelical-unity.

65   McCune, *Promise*, 114.

66   Ibid., 77–78. Iain Murray records the same incident and several other unfortunate, gospel-eroding comments from Billy Graham in *Evangelicalism Divided*, 64–69, 73–74. See also chapter 9 of Ernest Pickering's book *Biblical Separation: The Struggle for a Pure Church* (Schaumburg, IL: Regular Baptist Press, 1995), 141–55.

Jude wanted to fellowship, not fight. But the fight became *necessary* due to the presence of false teachers. I appreciate the way Kevin Bauder explains this: "We fellowship where we can. We separate where we must."[67]

Christians love unity. They pursue it. But in the face of heretical teaching, they cannot maintain unity—they must practice separation. And in this context, separation is *not* schism, despite unjust charges to the contrary. J. Gresham Machen was charged with schism in his day because he battled modernism, and he answered the accusation ably:

> Here, then, is the principle of the thing—it is schism to leave a church if that church is true to the Bible, but it is not schism if that church is not true to the Bible. In the latter case, far from its being schism to separate from the church in question, it is schism to remain in it, since to remain in it means to disobey the Word of God and to separate oneself from the true Church of Jesus Christ.[68]

My second point of clarification from Jude: Contrary to what I've generally heard from fundamentalists, the Bible's command when confronted with error is not necessarily to separate from it—it is to *fight* it. First fight, *then* flight—but only if the effort to purge impurities from within is unsuccessful.

It seems that at certain points in history, fundamentalists became so accustomed to losing battles that they stopped fighting them altogether, choosing instead to isolate themselves from the fray through a hasty separation. Further, they blamed orthodox brothers who continued to fight apostasy from within.[69] As a result, many fundamentalists blamed conservative Southern Baptists for staying in the embattled denomination when liberalism was exerting its influence in the 1960s and 70s. And they were confused and even offended when the conservative resurgence in the SBC actually *succeeded* in the 1980s and 90s. Our SBC brothers who were

---

67   Kevin Bauder, "Exhortation to 2006 Graduating Students," preached at Puritan Reformed Theological Seminary. tinysa.com/sermon/620619053.

68   J. Gresham Machen, "Are We Schismatics?" *Presbyterian Guardian*, 20 April 1936, 22.

69   Ernest Pickering wrote in 1979, "Church history yields no example of a group or denomination that, having been captured by apostates, has been rescued and restored to a Biblical witness." *Biblical Separation*, 160. I would argue that such a recovery—unprecedented and deemed virtually impossible by Pickering and others—*has happened* in the Southern Baptist Convention's conservative resurgence around 1979.

fighting error from within should have been prayed for and encouraged; instead, they were maligned.[70]

Now, I confess that I have become so tired of unbiblical schism that even biblically mandated separation has sometimes made me roll my eyes: *Not that again.* The doctrine of separation has been so misrepresented and misapplied that many are tempted to reject it altogether. I understand the temptation. But the damage that schism has done to the Bible's teaching about separation grieves me. Like Douglas McLachlan, I'm burdened to "rescue separation from some of the eccentricities which have gathered around it."[71] Despite missteps and abuses, the fight is necessary, and it won't be over until we reach heaven. Christians must not become indiscriminate. Love for the truth, love for the church, and love for the lost demand that we not only rejoice in the gospel but that we rally to its defense when it is opposed.

Gavin Ortlund's contrast of fundamentalists and liberals makes me smile: "There is no doctrine that a fundamentalist *won't* fight over, and no doctrine a liberal *will* fight over."[72] I've lived through examples of the former. An example of the latter is seen in a shocking statement from Episcopal bishop Peter James Lee in 2004:

> If you must make a choice between heresy and schism, always choose heresy. For as a heretic, you are only guilty of a wrong opinion. As a schismatic, you have torn and divided the body of Christ. Choose heresy every time.[73]

---

70   An example of this is David Beale's book *SBC: House on the Sand?* (Greenville, SC: Bob Jones University Press, 1985). Beale, one of my professors at BJU, correctly identified liberalism in Southern Baptist seminaries in the 1970s. But the call for conservatives to leave the SBC would have precluded the successful conservative resurgence which began in 1979 and purged SBC seminaries of liberalism. Separation is necessary, but only as a last resort. Praise God for a victory won in the SBC.

71   McLachlan, 117.

72   Gavin Ortlund, *Finding the Right Hills to Die On: The Case for Theological Triage* (Wheaton, IL: Crossway, 2020), 17.

73   Quoted by Allan Dobras in "Denominational Drift: The Bible Doesn't Need 'Rescuing,'" published by *BreakPoint* on April 11, 2006. This quote was drawn to my attention by Chuck Swindoll, *The Church Awakening: An Urgent Call for Renewal* (New York, NY: Faith Words, 2010), 62. Ironically, Swindoll was blacklisted as a new evangelical by most fundamentalists (myself included), but it was an inaccurate description since he has repudiated theological liberalism throughout his ministry. Notice how the esteemed D. Martin Lloyd-Jones argued, correctly, a generation earlier, for a priority exactly opposite of Bishop Lee's position: "Here is the great divide. The ecumenical people

Those who love Scripture can never "choose heresy." As we have seen, someone who separates over heresy is no schismatic. Unity must never displace purity as our priority. Some things are worth fighting over—and heresy tops the list. Much of this book is a critique of those who are too eager to fight. But the history of theological liberalism and of squishy evangelicalism reminds us of the need to fight for the truth.

This is important: *Contending and separating from apostasy isn't a distinctive of fundamentalism—it's a distinctive of faithful Christianity.* Hear this good word from Gavin Ortlund:

> Our theology must have a category for the censorious tone of Paul's letter to the Galatians and the grit and resolve of Machen's polemics. We must not reduce gospel witness to a generic niceness that is accommodating in every circumstance. There is a time to fight. There are certain hills that must not be surrendered, even if the cost is losing our lives.[74]

put fellowship before doctrine. We are evangelicals; we put doctrine before fellowship (Acts 2:42)." D. Martin Lloyd-Jones, *Knowing the Times: Addresses Delivered on Various Occasions 1942–77* (Edinburgh: Banner of Truth, 1989), 254.

74   Ortlund., 94.

CHAPTER 6

SCRIPTURE COMMANDS SEPARATION FROM UNREPENTANT CHRISTIANS

"Now we command you, brothers, in the name of our Lord Jesus Christ,
that you keep away from any brother who is walking in idleness
and not in accord with the tradition that you received from us."

—2 *Thessalonians* 3:6

Scripture commands separation from false teaching and false teachers. In contrast to the pluralism and ecumenism of our age, the Bible insists that to *tolerate* doctrinal heresy is to *promote* doctrinal heresy.

But more controversial by far is the idea that Scripture calls us to separate from unrepentant Christians who are engaged in grievous sins. This is where confusion reigns. And here we face two perils: Those who *refuse to separate* from perpetually sinful Christians are neglecting and breaking repeated Bible commands.[75] But those who seem to *take pleasure in separating* from fellow believers "for any cause" (to repurpose Matthew 19:3) run the risk of unbiblical schism. The Bible position is in the middle of those two ditches, and it's prominent in the New Testament—not just a "fine-print" mention.

---

75   Rolland McCune writes, "The Bible teaches separation from Christians who are doctrinally careless or who are content to walk with those who deny the faith." Rolland McCune, *Ecclesiastical Separation* (Detroit, MI: Detroit Baptist Theological Seminary, n.d.), 4. I agree with McCune, though we need to maintain the sort of doctrinal triage which early fundamentalists employed; not all doctrinal differences arise from carelessness. Similarly, McCune's insistence that brothers with whom we fellowship must avoid cooperation with apostates is essential, but extending the guilt-by-association chain too far becomes unhelpful.

The passages in the New Testament that outline how and why Christians must sometimes break fellowship with other Christians essentially deal with what we call "church discipline." The focus is on how an individual local church addresses an unrepentant church member. I will argue that these passages also establish principles for how to deal with unrepentant believers outside of the local church setting, but the primary context is certainly within the local church.

Mark Dever and his 9Marks ministry have done a great job advocating for biblical church discipline in recent years. Dever lists five reasons why church discipline is essential.

1. For the good of the person disciplined
2. For the good of the other Christians, as they see the danger of sin
3. For the health of the church as a whole
4. For the corporate witness of the church
5. For the glory of God, as we reflect His holiness[76]

I've walked through church discipline, and it's always exercised with grief. I remember my reluctance to discipline a young lady in our church who had moved in with her boyfriend. Despite our efforts to recover her from her error, she was unrepentant. Though she clearly required discipline, I was tempted to wait because her mother was battling terminal cancer at the time. Remarkably, it was her mother who ultimately urged me to remove the young lady from church membership, both for her daughter's good and the church's. I did so, and her mother and I both wept through the members meetings.

I remember another time when we moved toward discipline with two church leaders who had attempted a *coup* during a members meeting. I'll never forget the courage of my fellow elders who rallied around me, confronted the schismatic brothers, and thereby preserved the unity—and perhaps the very existence—of our young church by confronting the erring brothers and insisting that they repent if they wanted to remain at the church. (They did not.)

This issue is difficult, but Scripture is clear that sometimes church unity *needs* to be disrupted.

---

76   Mark Dever, *Nine Marks of a Healthy Church* (Wheaton, IL: Crossway Books, 2004), 188–90.

In order to deal with this difficult topic carefully, I'm going to move con-secutively through five New Testament passages that call us to separate from or discipline unrepentant sinful Christians. Each time I will note (1) the description of the offender, (2) the nature of the offense, and (3) the biblically mandated response. See if you can trace Dever's reasons for disci-pline in each of the passages.

Jesus' Command to Separate from Unrepentant Brothers (Matthew 18:15–17)

This is a classic passage on church discipline and one of only two texts in the four Gospels that use the word "church" (the other being Matthew 16:18).

> If your brother sins against you, go and tell him his fault, between you and him alone. If he listens to you, you have gained your brother. But if he does not listen, take one or two others along with you, that every charge may be established by the evidence of two or three witnesses. If he refuses to listen to them, tell it to the church. And if he refuses to listen even to the church, let him be to you as a Gentile and a tax collector. (Matthew 18:15–17)

1. *The Description of the Offender:* Matthew 18:15 calls the offender "your brother." So, this is a fellow Christian, or at least a professing Christian. To be clear, "brother" in this passage is a generic term for a fellow Christian—not just a male. The offending person could be a brother or a sister in the church.

2. *The Nature of the Offense:* Matthew 18:15 simply says this fellow Christian "sins against you." The offense is unnamed, so the passage gives us a template for *any* significant offense that causes a disruption of fellow-ship between believers. Minor offenses can be covered by godly forbear-ance. But if a Christian relationship is broken—by gossip, dishonesty, immorality, or another practice Scripture clearly forbids—it needs to be addressed as Jesus commands. Notice that Jesus' instructions are general and proactive, anticipating problems that would arise among believers in the future.

3. *The Biblically Mandated Response:* Matthew 18:15–17 outlines a series of steps that you are to take to "gain your brother" (v. 15). Note that the goal is reconciliation, not retribution or retaliation. If your goal isn't restored

fellowship, check your own heart before confronting the brother. De-log your own eye so you can de-speck your brother's (Matthew 7:3–5). That said, the Bible commands you to go to your brother, tell him his fault, and do so between just the two of you. It's almost comical how much trouble Jesus goes through to prevent gossip. He knows our frame! He commands you to go to *your brother/sister* (not someone else)…to tell *him/her* (and nobody else) the fault…between you and *him/her* (not another)…*alone!* Clear enough? Ideally, this offending person will see his or her error, repent, and your fellowship will be restored. You can stop the entire process in verse 15—no one else needs to know. It's time to rejoice, give thanks to God, and move on.

But there are times when your brother will resist your efforts and continue in his sinful posture. At that point, Scripture calls for a "bigger hammer," so to speak: go back to the person with one or two others, preferably church leaders who can serve as peacemakers (v. 16). If he or she repents at this point, praise the Lord. That's as far as it has to go.

Sadly, sinning Christians sometimes refuse to listen even to church leaders. At this point, an even bigger hammer appears: "tell it to the church" (v. 17). Hopefully the shame of having the sin exposed to the entire body will inspire repentance and bring about reconciliation.

Too often, however, matters that reach the point of full-church involvement seem inevitably to progress to the last step: discipline out of church membership. At this point, the offender has given no evidence of true Christianity. As a result, the entire church (not just the leaders) is to treat the person as an unbeliever. This doesn't mean that we are to be vicious. But it does require that we restrict normal Christian fellowship as opposed to carrying on as though all were well. We shift to evangelizing this person and praying for his conversion and/or recovery.

Matthew 18 sets the tone for the entire discipline/separation discussion. The apostolic passages that follow must all be read in light of these words from our Savior. Yes, at times breaks in Christian fellowship are necessary. But they are a last resort, and they need not be final. As Fred Moritz writes, "There is no scriptural justification for hasty separation which is not preceded by repeated attempts to reconcile estranged brethren and to restore the erring brother."[77]

Paul's Command to Separate from Deceitful Brothers (Romans 16:17–18)

Paul's teaching on discipline/separation in the book of Romans is concise, but it is important—especially because one of the book's main purposes is to promote Christian unity. In order to preserve true unity, the church must "avoid" those who promote schism contrary to Scripture.

> I appeal to you, brothers, to watch out for those who cause divisions and create obstacles contrary to the doctrine that you have been taught; avoid them. For such persons do not serve our Lord Christ, but their own appetites, and by smooth talk and flattery they deceive the hearts of the naïve. (Romans 16:17–18)

1. *The Description of the Offender:* Romans 16:17 warns against trouble-making "brothers"—those within the church at Rome. Again, the word references Christians in general, male and female.

2. *The Nature of the Offense:* The Christians in question are guilty of causing divisions and creating obstacles. Their disruption of unity has a doctrinal focus—they are promoting concepts "contrary to the doctrine that you have been taught." These are professing Christians who are teaching heresies. In our day, common heresies might include a denial of human sinfulness, a rejection of God's wrath, annihilationism, unbiblical concepts of sexuality and gender, and so on.

    Romans 16:18 provides more details regarding the rabblerousers' sin. They were serving their own appetites rather than the Lord Jesus. There was a selfish motive behind their divisiveness. Finally, the sinning brothers or sisters seem to have targeted immature Christians with deceptive speech: "by smooth talk and flattery they deceive the hearts of the naïve." One of the primary motives of church discipline is to prevent the leaven-like spread of sin in the church.

---

77   Fred Moritz, "Be Ye Holy": *The Call to Christian Separation* (Greenville, SC: Bob Jones University Press, 1994), 81. Gregory and Gregory similarly insist that faithful believers will never "rejoice" over separation, but "will mourn the breaking of unity that separation always produces. Severance from relationship will be a last resort." Gregory and Gregory, 152.

3. *The Biblically Mandated Response:* Paul's instructions to the church regarding those causing church divisions are succinct: "Avoid them." Rather than calling for a passive-aggressive cold shoulder at church potlucks, this is likely a call to officially put the unrepentant members out of the church.

Paul's Command to Separate from Immoral Brothers (1 Corinthians 5)

The Corinthian church was a holy mess. We'll deal with it in more detail in chapter 10. But 1 Corinthians 5 gives us an example of just how carnal a church can be. Here, Paul gives the most extensive treatment of discipline of or separation from a professing Christian in the Scriptures.

It is actually reported that there is sexual immorality among you, and of a kind that is not tolerated even among pagans, for a man has his father's wife. And you are arrogant! Ought you not rather to mourn? Let him who has done this be removed from among you. For though absent in body, I am present in spirit; and as if present, I have already pronounced judgment on the one who did such a thing. When you are assembled in the name of the Lord Jesus and my spirit is present, with the power of our Lord Jesus, you are to deliver this man to Satan for the destruction of the flesh, so that his spirit may be saved in the day of the Lord. Your boasting is not good. Do you not know that a little leaven leavens the whole lump? Cleanse out the old leaven that you may be a new lump, as you really are unleavened. For Christ, our Passover lamb, has been sacrificed. Let us therefore celebrate the festival, not with the old leaven, the leaven of malice and evil, but with the unleavened bread of sincerity and truth. I wrote to you in my letter not to associate with sexually immoral people—not at all meaning the sexually immoral of this world, or the greedy and swindlers, or idolaters, since then you would need to go out of the world. But now I am writing to you not to associate with anyone who bears the name of brother if he is guilty of sexual immorality or greed, or is an idolater, reviler, drunkard, or swindler—not even to eat with such a one. For what have I to do with judging outsiders? Is it not those inside the church whom you are to judge? God judges those outside. "Purge the evil person from among you." (1 Corinthians 5:1–13)

1. *The Description of the Offender:* Paul writes to the Corinthian church about sin "among you" (v. 1). The fact that the person in question was a professing Christian is clarified later in the chapter, where Paul explains that he is *not* calling for separation from unbelievers, "since then you would need to go out of the world" (v. 9). Instead, he calls for discipline/separation when one "who bears the name of brother" (v. 11) and who is "inside the church" (v. 12) is living in grievous and unrepentant sin. Notice that the professing brother is called an "evil person" (v. 13), which brings the reality of his own conversion into question.

2. *The Nature of the Offense:* There are two scandals that Paul addresses in this passage. The first is a sin so outrageous that even the pagan idolaters in the city of Corinth were shocked: "It is actually reported that there is sexual immorality among you, and of a kind that is not tolerated even among pagans, for a man has his father's wife" (v. 1). The second scandal is the church's proud toleration of the sin: "And you are arrogant! Ought you not rather to mourn?" (v. 2).

However, Paul moves beyond this specific and rather outrageous circumstance and uses it as an example of how all churches should deal with other grievous sins. He speaks both of this man and of "anyone" (v. 11) who is a professing believer and yet engaged in immorality, making this man an example for similar cases. Indeed, he expands the discussion further with other hypothetical scenarios, including a professing Christian who is "guilty of…greed, or is an idolater, reviler, drunkard, or swindler" (v. 11). The sins listed, including the incest, are clearly exemplary, not exhaustive.

3. *The Biblically Mandated Response:* Paul's instructions to the Corinthians are very precise. The brother in question must be "removed from among you" (v. 2). The church cannot stop him from sinning, but it can stop the mockery of treating him like a member in good standing. Removal from the church brings with it removal from the church's spiritual oversight and protection: "Deliver this man to Satan for the destruction of the flesh" (v. 5a). What a frightening description of discipline! However, the hope is that allowing the brother to sin in isolation from the church will lead to conviction and repentance: "so that his spirit may be saved in the day of the Lord" (v. 5b).

Paul calls for the "leaven" of sin to be removed before the entire "loaf" of the church is contaminated (v. 7). He gives still more detailed commands, ordering the church "not to associate" with such a person (vv. 9, 11). Normal relationships are to be suspended until repentance is gained. Paul's next gives the politically incorrect command for the church to "judge" the sinner (v. 12)—to reach an unmistakable verdict. As though he had not yet made himself clear, Paul concludes with yet one more expression for discipline/separation: "Purge the evil person from among you" (v. 13). This separation/discipline is once again the action of the entire church (presumably through an official vote during a congregational meeting), not just of the church's leaders.

Paul's Command to Separate from Lazy Brothers (2 Thessalonians 3:6–15)

Like the churches in Rome and Corinth, the church in Thessalonica had professing Christians who were guilty of unrepentant sin. The text addresses laziness, but it broadens to other sins that reveal unsound doctrine.

> Now we command you, brothers, in the name of our Lord Jesus Christ, that you keep away from any brother who is walking in idleness and not in accord with the tradition that you received from us. For you yourselves know how you ought to imitate us, because we were not idle when we were with you, nor did we eat anyone's bread without paying for it, but with toil and labor we worked night and day, that we might not be a burden to any of you. It was not because we do not have that right, but to give you in ourselves an example to imitate. For even when we were with you, we would give you this command: If anyone is not willing to work, let him not eat. For we hear that some among you walk in idleness, not busy at work, but busybodies. Now such persons we command and encourage in the Lord Jesus Christ to do their work quietly and to earn their own living. As for you, brothers, do not grow weary in doing good. If anyone does not obey what we say in this letter, take note of that person, and have nothing to do with him, that he may be ashamed. Do not regard him as an enemy, but warn him as a brother. (2 Thessalonians 3:6–15)

1. *The Description of the Offender:* This text again addresses a Christian "brother" (v. 6)—one who is "among you" (v. 11). The church is to treat the sinning party "as a brother" and not "as an enemy" (v. 15). We're dealing with a professing Christian.

2. *The Nature of the Offense:* Verses 6, 7, and 13 focus on the immediate sin faced by the Thessalonian church: failure of professing Christians to work. Due to a faulty eschatology that taught that Jesus' return would be so immediate that normal work was unnecessary, Christians were refusing to work to support themselves and their families—an issue Paul had already addressed with this very church in 1 Thessalonians 4:11–12. So, wrong *belief* and neglect of apostolic teaching fostered wrong *behavior*.

   That said, verses 6 and 14 seem to expand the discussion beyond failure to work to more general behavioral problems that are out of step with apostolic teaching.[78] Thus, as in 1 Corinthians 5, the issue at hand is exemplary, not exhaustive.

3. *The Biblically Mandated Response:* The first command is to "keep away from" the erring believer (v. 6). Verse 10 commands the church to stop enabling this brother in his sin by rewarding his laziness with financial bailouts. Verse 14 tells the church to "take note" of him and "have nothing to do with him," reiterating the "keep away" command of verse 6. The goal of the discipline is that the brother will be ashamed of his misconduct and repent (v. 14). The restorative goal of discipline/separation is expressed again in verse 15: "Do not regard him as an enemy, but warn him as a brother." Church discipline is corrective in its intent, not punitive.

Paul's Command to Separate from Schismatic Brothers (Titus 3:10–11)

Titus 3 offers us another interesting example of church discipline. Many Christians—if they see the need for church discipline at all—might assume that it's for the kind of sexual deviancy mentioned in 1 Corinthians 5. But

---

78   Bruce Compton sees the instructions in 2 Thessalonians 3 as exemplary as well: "By application, any conscious violation of a specific command given to them by the apostle would qualify the offender for the same discipline directed in verse 6." R. Bruce Compton, "2 Thessalonians 3:6–15 and Biblical Separation," *The Sentinel*, Fall 1988, 20.

Titus 3 instructs the church not to tolerate a person who is stubbornly *divisive*—a sin as serious in God's mind as gross immorality.

> As for a person who stirs up division, after warning him once and then twice, have nothing more to do with him, knowing that such a person is warped and sinful; he is self-condemned. (Titus 3:10–11)

1. *The Description of the Offender:* The offending party is clearly a member of the church. This person may be one who is guilty of the pointless arguments Paul mentions in verse 9: the instruction to avoid "foolish controversies, genealogies, dissensions, and quarrels" leads naturally to the separation commands in verses 10 and 11.

2. *The Nature of the Offense:* The sinning brother or sister in this instance is a schismatic—one who "stirs up division." The King James Version calls the person a "heretic," a transliteration of the Greek word *hairetikos*. However, the English term *heretic* connotes one guilty of heresy or false teaching, and it's unlikely that that's what's happening in Titus 3. A full-fledged false teacher would not be warned repeatedly but would be immediately put out of the church (2 John 10–11). Instead, the person in question is one who is sinfully divisive. He is clearly unteachable, as the two warnings have had no effect. This is a character problem, not merely a spiritual misstep. The divisive brother "is warped and sinful; he is self-condemned" (v. 11).

3. *The Biblically Mandated Response:* The church's responsibility when faced with an unteachable troublemaker is to give two warnings, then to "have nothing more to do with him." Whereas we conceive of church discipline as a button we push only for such scandals as adultery, Scripture commands us to exercise it when a person is stirring up division. As ironic as it may sound, *unbiblical separation—schism—may necessitate biblical separation.* Were we to obey Scripture on this point, schism would be far less common.

Do Church Discipline Passages Apply Outside of the Local Church?

All of these passages deal with church discipline. The question many will pose is whether they should also be applied to Christians' relationships with other professing believers outside of their local church. I believe the answer to be *yes*, and Rolland McCune explains the rationale well:

If disregard for the word of God qualified people for dismissal from the fellowship of a local church, on what basis could there be broader organizational fellowship with them, even in a worthy project such as winning others to Christ? The polity that regulates local church fellowship also in principle regulates ecclesiastical connections and associations that may transcend the affairs of a local church. Paul explicitly named two Christian leaders who had deviated in doctrine and conscience and who were consequently "handed over to Satan" (1 Tim 1:20). This means at least excision from the local assembly, but a warning for all other pastors and churches is implicit.[79]

The difference, of course, is that local churches have an innate authority granted them in the Bible—one that doesn't exist in other associations or personal relationships. Denominations, mission boards, and seminaries have an agreed-upon authority structure, which is useful, albeit extrabiblical. But the same errors that necessitate discipline at the local church level also warrant separation at other levels. It may be as unofficial as John Piper's "Farewell, Rob Bell" tweet that indicated that Bell's heretical teaching inevitably put him outside the bounds of biblical orthodoxy (and thereby outside the bounds of evangelical fellowship, at least with Piper).[80] But it will often be more formal.

When it comes to issues like platform fellowship, associational membership, and even collaborations like writing projects, a brother who is in serious and unrepentant error cannot be embraced by other flawed-but-faithful believers. Historically, that has meant that a legitimate brother who engages in ecumenical meetings will therefore not be allowed to engage in meetings with *me*. Similarly, a brother who believes the gospel but who caves on the issue of homosexuality, gender identity, or female pastors won't be a brother I collaborate with in ministry endeavors. It's a valid principle, and one that I practice—though the guilt-by-association argument often described as "secondary separation" can quickly degenerate into a ludicrous chain reaction.[81]

---

79   McCune, *Promise*, 150.

80   twitter.com/JohnPiper/status/41590656421863424.

81   It is worth noting that fundamentalists have never been in lockstep agreement on secondary separation. John R. Rice, while editor of *The Sword of the Lord*, practiced biblical separation but repudiated secondary separation: "No, there are no Scriptures that we can find which teach that we ought to separate from those who do not separate from those who do not do everything we think

Of course, the goal is not constant conflict. We must resist the creation of a "Christian cancel culture" anytime someone disagrees with us on a relatively minor issue. And we must resist the temptation to separate from every Christian who doesn't draw the lines of separation and fellowship precisely where we do. I've seen that kind of quick-triggered separation from those who are several degrees removed from actual error. Such folly is not in line with the passages discussed above and throws the entire doctrine of separation into ill repute. I appreciate this counsel from Don Bixby: "Considering the importance of unity, the decision to separate must be supported by clear Biblical principle or risk divine censure for being illegitimately factious."[82]

Still, we must be willing to break fellowship when Scripture requires it. When a serious error becomes a habit rather than a misstep, Scripture calls for separation even from otherwise orthodox brothers.

In chapter two, I compared separation from fellow believers to amputation. It's not something we should celebrate or embrace as our defining identity. But amputations are sometimes necessary to preserve a life. They are grievous, to be sure, and they are a last resort. Try spiritual antibiotics. Try surgery. But Christians must sometimes separate from other Christians—not hastily or happily, but obediently. When we must do so, let's be careful to proceed with the patience and caution Scripture requires.

---

they should. Secondary separation is nowhere clearly taught in the Scriptures." John R. Rice, *Come Out—Or Stay In?* (Nashville, TN: Thomas Nelson, Inc., 1974), 226. Interestingly, he made his case using multiple modern Bible versions.

82   Don W. Bixby, "Separation in Search of Balance," class paper at Central Baptist Theological Seminary, 1990, 29.

CHAPTER 7

JESUS' PASSION FOR LOVING UNITY

"Rather, speaking the truth in love, we are to grow up in every way into him who is the head, into Christ."

—Ephesians 4:15

Christians tend to be lovers or fighters. Some have such a longing for unity that they are prone to tolerate serious error. Others are so burdened for purity that they can become unapologetically harsh. I'm not saying that every believer lives in one ditch or the other—but I do think one comes more naturally to most of us than the other. In Luther's words, "Softness and hardness are the two main faults from which all the mistakes of pastors come."[83]

Scripture's ideal is a combination of the two. We want a *pure unity*—a *unified purity*. I often challenge Christians, "You don't have to be a cactus to stand up straight. Be an oak!" It is indeed possible to be relentlessly committed to the truth while simultaneously prioritizing biblical love. Paul taught the Ephesians that "speaking the truth in love" is how Christians "grow up in every way into him who is the head, into Christ" (Ephesians 4:15). In fact, Paul's teaching about healthy church life in Ephesians 4:1–16 *repeatedly* emphasizes both doctrinal purity and unyielding unity.

For many years, I tended to emphasize purity to the neglect of unity. Were I able to talk to my younger, schismatic self, I'd tell him that *love* and *unity*

---

83   Martin Luther, *Luther's Works*, ed. Hilton C. Oswald (St. Louis, MO: Concordia, 1972), 25:139.

are at the core of true biblical Christianity as surely as sound doctrine is. But don't take my word for it. Listen to our Savior.

Go back with me to the upper room, 2,000 years ago. Jesus is just hours away from enduring the horrors of Gethsemane, the betrayal of His disciples, and the indignity of an illegal all-night trial. He is on the precipice of Calvary's abyss, where He would be crucified by sinners and crushed by His Father. By enduring God's wrath in the place of sinners, He would accomplish the very purpose for which He came to Earth as planned within the Trinity in eternity past. It was a night like no other. And in those epic hours, Jesus repeatedly called His disciples to *love* and *unity*.

Years ago, I wrote a little devotional called *Sundown to Sundown* about the twenty-four hours that preceded Christ's death. In those final hours before the atonement, every moment counted. Jesus washed the disciples' feet. He comforted them with the promise of the outpouring of the Spirit. He instituted the Lord's Table and initiated the New Covenant. He warned them that they would abandon Him, though the warnings would go unheeded.

And He bookended all of it by *speaking to them* in John 13 and *praying for them* in John 17. His command was to "love one another" and His prayer request was "that they may be one."

Jesus' Command: "Love One Another" (John 13)

Jesus began the time in the upper room in a remarkable way. Despite the strain that would cause Him to kneel and agonize in the garden just a few hours later, Jesus set aside His own needs even as He set aside His garments. He did the most menial of tasks, not only because the washing of feet had been neglected, but because He was determined to teach His disciples a life-changing lesson about humility.

The climax of John 13 isn't Jesus' washing the disciples' feet, however. It's not even His call for the disciples to humble themselves and serve each other. The climax of John 13 is Jesus' command in verses 34 and 35:

> A new commandment I give to you, that you love one another: just as I have loved you, you also are to love one another. By this all people will know that you are my disciples, if you have love for one another.

What a remarkable charge, issued at a remarkable time. Those two sentences are so pregnant with meaning that they are still being unpacked and applied two millennia later.

Jesus commands us to love each other as He has loved us. The command to love each other wasn't new. The second great commandment is to love our neighbors as ourselves, and it had been in play for 1,500 years at that point (Matthew 22:34–40, citing Leviticus 19:18). But Jesus infinitely raises the bar: "Don't just love each other the way *you* love you—love each other the way *I* have loved you." Jesus repeats this command in John 15:12–13, specifically linking our love for others to our willingness to imitate His self-sacrifice: "This is my commandment, that you love one another as I have loved you. Greater love has no one than this, that someone lay down his life for his friends." He repeats the command yet again in John 15:17: "These things I command you, so that you will love one another."

The passion of Christ is my favorite topic for meditation. I think often of Jesus' suffering on our behalf. I write frequently about it; my best hymn lyrics focus on Jesus' sacrifice for sinners. But rarely do I look at Jesus' suffering on the cross as a model of the way I should love other Christians. I focus on the doctrinal significance of the vicarious atonement—and that *is* primary. But Jesus also commands us to view His bloody sacrifice as an example to emulate as we love one another. Paul does the same in Philippians 2:1–11, citing Jesus' shocking condescension to a scandalous death on a cross as a template for our loving unity. This deserves more of my attention, and I suspect more of yours as well. When we think about Jesus' death for us, we should then think about our love for fellow Christians.

Think on 1 John 4:11: "Beloved, if God so loved us, we also ought to love one another." Let's unpack that if/then statement a bit. "*If God* (the sinless One; the high and lofty One; the all-wise One; the thrice-holy One) *so loved us* (His enemies; rebels; faithless and fickle sinners), *then we also ought to love one another* (our fellow creatures and fellow Christians; our brothers and sisters; our partners in vice, and often, our superiors in virtue). Do you not see the atrocity of withholding the love you've so undeservedly received? As Hugh Binning asks, "If all that was in me did not alienate [God's] love from me, how should any thing in others estrange our love to them?"[84]

---

84   Binning, 32.

The entire Christian ethic is essentially our extending to others what we have received from God—our "recycling" of what we call God's communicable attributes. We love as we've been loved, forgive as we've been forgiven, comfort as we've been comforted, and so on. Our love is possible only because we have first been loved and have been transformed from our innate selfishness by that love. We love *because* God loves, and we are to love *like* God loves.

Thus, Jim Berg describes biblical love this way: "Cultivating a God-imitating mindset that scripturally and sacrificially advances the spiritual welfare of others."[85] The description may not put a tear in your eye, but it's profound. Biblical love imitates our Savior. It is self-sacrificing. It seeks others' spiritual good—it seeks their discipleship, their growth, their service, and their joy.

Do you love like that? Does anyone you know love like that? Can you imagine being part of a *church* that loves like that?! It would be peaceful. It would be mature. And it would be unified. I like how Margaret Mitchell describes the role of love in Christ's church: If the church is a spiritual building, love is "the mortar between the bricks" that holds the church together.[86]

Jesus commands us to love each other as a testimony to the world. John 13:34–35 teaches that the world will know that we're Christians by our love for each other, a concept repeated in John 17:21. Francis Schaeffer called love and unity "the final apologetic"—Jesus' ultimate proof of His ministry and our identity as His disciples.[87] But is love what the world sees when they look at the church today? Hardly. Francis Chan, with characteristic punch, describes how our lack of love comes off to the watching world:

> Have you ever considered how outsiders must view us? Try to imagine
> an unbeliever going online and trying to make sense of all the different

---

85   Jim Berg, *Essential Virtues: Marks of the Christ-Centered Life* (Greenville, SC: JourneyForth, 2008), 132. While this description of love focuses on the fixed will of the lover that determines to love even the unlovely, this in no way removes the concept of emotion or deep *affection* from either God's love or the Christian's love, as D. A. Carson demonstrates in *The Difficult Doctrine of the Love of God* (Wheaton, IL: Crossway, 2000), 58–64.

86   Margaret M. Mitchell, *Paul and the Rhetoric of Reconciliation: An Exegetical Investigation* (Louisville, KY: Westminster/John Knox Press, 1993), 171. Disclaimer: I like this particular quote, not Mitchell's theology.

87   Schaeffer, 163 and 171.

denominations, church splits, competitive advertising, and open slander. It would look like my family screaming frantically at each other while walking through an orphanage to meet kids wanting adoption. There is a reason people aren't anxious to join our family.[88]

We have no excuse for our scandalous lack of love. Jesus commanded us to love each other; then *He showed us what bloody sacrificial love looks like* by His sacrificial and saving death on the cross. Although it took them a while, the apostles *got it.* No wonder they emphasized love as the apex of Christian virtue throughout the New Testament.

Peter commands us to "love one another earnestly from a pure heart" (1 Peter 1:22). Notice that love and purity are inseparable, not mutually exclusive. He goes on to say that such love is an evidence that we've been born again (1 Peter 1:23). He tells us to "love the brotherhood" (1 Peter 2:17). He urges us to "have unity of mind, sympathy, brotherly love, a tender heart, and a humble mind" in our relationships (1 Peter 3:8). And he insists that—"above all"—we "keep loving one another earnestly, since love covers a multitude of sins" (1 Peter 4:8).

John tells us—again and again and again—that love is so central to the Christian life that one who doesn't love fellow believers is no Christian at all (1 John 2:15; 3:10, 11, 14, 16, 17, 18, 23; 4:7, 8, 11, 12, 16, 19, 20, 21; 5:2).

Paul shows us the gritty nature of biblical love by elevating it above even miraculous spiritual gifts, calling it the "greatest" virtue, and arguing that loveless works are but a nuisance (1 Corinthians 13). We could summarize "the love chapter" as follows: *Love endures the worst and assumes the best.* Paul tells us to "let all that [we] do be done in love" (1 Corinthians 16:14). He says that love is the fulfillment of the law (Galatians 5:14; see Romans 13:8–10). He lists love as the first and primary fruit of the Spirit (Galatians 5:22–23). He commands us to "bear with one another in love," to "speak the truth in love," to "build [each other] up in love," and to "walk in love, as Christ loved us and gave himself up for us" (Ephesians 4:2, 15–16; 5:2). He prays that our love will "increase and abound" (1 Thessalonians 3:12).

But the extensive emphasis on loving others throughout Jesus' words to His disciples and in the apostles' own writings reiterates that every Christian should strive to treat other believers—imperfect as they are—with the same

---

88   Francis Chan, *Until Unity* (Colorado Springs, CO: David C. Cook, 2021), 26.

humble and sacrificial love that we've been shown by our selfless, bloodied Savior. Jesus commanded and exemplified such love.

And He prayed for our unity.

Jesus' Prayer: "That They May Be One" (John 17)

I come now to Jesus' high priestly prayer in John 17, and I address it with some reluctance. Who can do justice to the depth of meaning and feeling we witness as we eavesdrop on the Son's communion with the Father? John 17 is holy ground. But it was inspired and recorded for our benefit, so we do well to study it, despite our wonder.

Jesus, hours from His own death, prays first for Himself, then for His disciples, and finally for those who would believe in Him through their witness—the church of all ages. And His primary concern for His people is that we should be "*kept*" (vv. 11, 12, 15). Why this precise request?

First, Jesus had "kept" the disciples during His earthly ministry (v. 12), despite their frailty. None had been lost but Judas. But now He was departing to return to the Father. The Father and Son were not yet sending the Holy Spirit in His unique New Testament capacity. And so, Jesus commits the care of His disciples to the Father: *Keep them.*

He prays that we would be kept from the world. Indeed, the fact that Jesus distinguishes His disciples from the world is instructive: "I am praying for them. I am not praying for the world but for those whom you have given me, for they are yours" (John 17:9). Here, as throughout the New Testament, God's people are distinguished from the unbelieving world— *not* from each other. We are to be kept from the world (v. 11). We are to be kept from evil (v. 15). And we are to be kept *together*—to be "one" just as the Father, Son, and Spirit are one. What remarkable words!

Jesus' prayer is that our togetherness, our unity, would be an extension of the unity shared eternally by the Trinity. We are to be "one" as the Trinity are one—not only in imitation or reflection, but in intimate fellowship both with the Triune God and with one another. We are "in" Them in some mysterious union (v. 21). *Get this! The unity of Christ's church is an extension of the very unity of the Trinity.* I can't begin to understand that, much less explain it. But our mysterious union with the Father, Son, and Spirit provides and necessitates union with other Christians. Edmund Clowney notes, "It is unity with God that creates that unity of God's people."[89]

In praying for unity, Jesus essentially prays that we would be preserved from *ourselves*. He asks for unity, as opposed to the schismatic infighting that is inherent in our human nature, that was evident among the twelve disciples even on that epic evening, and that has been too common throughout church history. *Deliver us from us!*

My favorite commentator on the four Gospels is the Anglican preacher J. C. Ryle, a contemporary of Spurgeon's. Ryle's comments on Jesus' prayer for our unity in John 17:11 are profound:

> Here our Lord mentions one special object for which He desires that His people may be kept: viz., their unity: that they may be one.—"Keep them, that they may be of one heart and one mind, striving together against common foes and for common ends, and not broken up, weakened, and paralyzed by internal quarrels and divisions"....
>
> The importance attached by our Lord to "unity" among Christians, is very strikingly illustrated in the prominent place assigned to it in this verse. The very first object for which He desires the preservation of the disciples, is that they may be kept from division. Nor can we wonder at this, when we consider the interminable divisions of Christians in every age, the immense harm they have done in the world, and the astounding indifference with which many regard them, as if they were perfectly innocent things, and as if the formation of new sects was a laudable work![90]

Of course, the prayer for unity is only part of Jesus' prayer, not all of it. He also prays for our purity—"Sanctify them in the truth; your word is truth" (v. 17; see v. 19). Jesus was no advocate of "peace at any price." He taught that we can be both *orthodox* and *loving*—both *sanctified* and *unified*. Both are essential.

---

89   Edmund P. Clowney, *The Church* (Downers Grove, IL: InterVarsity Press, 1995), 79.

90   J. C. Ryle, *Expository Thoughts on the Gospels: John 10:31 – John 21:25* (Grand Rapids, MI: Baker Book House, 2007), 189.

"Speaking the Truth in Love"

I opened this chapter by noting that most Christians are more naturally drawn toward either truth *or* love, purity *or* unity. The either/or tendency was certainly true in my experience.

During my ministry training and early pastorate, there was a perpetual drumbeat calling Christians to separation—but without a proportional drumbeat calling Christians to love and unity. In fact, calls for unity in Scripture almost *annoyed* me. Passages like John 13 and John 17 struck me almost as unfortunate. Like, why'd Jesus have to say *that?!*

And so, I'd intentionally deemphasize love and unity. For all practical purposes, I basically filtered the Lord Jesus! I avoided John 13 and John 17. Truly. And if I did cite them, I immediately worked to undermine them. *"Jesus commanded us to love each other, BUT...." "Jesus prayed for unity, BUT...."* There was always an immediate qualification. *"Jesus wasn't promoting ecumenism"* or *"Jesus wasn't neglecting holiness"* or *"Jesus wasn't calling for compromise"* or *"These verses have been twisted by the modern church."* It was like I was afraid of the very words of Christ—as if *I* knew better. And yet, despite my arrogant protestations, Jesus *did* command us to love each other. Hard stop. Jesus *did* pray for our unity. Hard stop.

But He wasn't finished. Jesus literally *died* to accomplish that unity. Read that again: *Jesus died so that Christians would be at peace with one another.* Ephesians 2:14–16 says so, describing how Jesus' death accomplished peace not only between sinners and God but between sinners and other sinners—in context, Jewish Christians and Gentile Christians:

> For he himself is our peace, who has made us both one and has broken down in his flesh the dividing wall of hostility by abolishing the law of commandments expressed in ordinances, that he might create in himself one new man in place of the two, so making peace, and might reconcile us both to God in one body through the cross, thereby killing the hostility.[91]

"Through the cross." Please let that sink in. Jesus commanded us to love each other. Jesus prayed for our unity. And then Jesus went to the *cross* to reconcile us to God and to one another.

---

91   My friend Dean Taylor does a masterful job unpacking this text in chapter two of his book *The Thriving Church: The True Measure of Growth* (Greenville, SC: JourneyForth, 2019), 31–47.

It must be important.

You Made Us One

You made us one, Creator God—
Formed in Your image by Your Son.
One human race, with common blood—
We are diverse, yet we are one.

Sin made us one, O holy God;
We sinned in Adam and like Eve.
We share our crimes, not just our blood—
Joined in our fall, our guilt, our need.

Grace makes us one, redeeming God—
One holy church through faith in Christ.
Spirit-indwelt, washed by Your blood—
From ev'ry nation, tongue and tribe.

Chorus

As You are one, O Three-in-One,
We are united through Your Son!
You made us one, as You are one.[92]

---

92   Lyrics from "You Made Us One" by Chris Anderson and Richard A. Nichols. ©2022 Church
      Works Worship (ASCAP) (adm at IntegratedRights.com). All rights reserved. Used by permission.
      Download a free version: churchworksmedia.com/product/you-made-us-one-free.

‹ PART 3 ›

WHEN SEPARATION IS SINFUL

"The plight of the Christian church seems almost as sad as that of the world. To all appearances it, too, is a house divided against itself. It resembles a beautiful vase that, fallen from its perch, lies shattered in a thousand pieces. It is like a grand structure transformed by an exploding bomb into a tangled heap of wreckage. Unbelievable though it may seem, the church of Jesus Christ is really one."

—R. B. Kuiper[93]

---

93   Kuiper, 41.

CHAPTER 8

DIOTREPHES AND SCHISMATIC AMBITION

"Diotrephes, who likes to put himself first,
does not acknowledge our authority."

—3 John 9

When is the last time you heard or preached a sermon on 2 or 3 John? Both are underappreciated books of Scripture. They're short—two of the four one-chapter letters of the New Testament. They're basically postcards. But they're so rich, teaching vital lessons about religious alliances, God-glorifying missions, and the role we get to play in gospel expansion. Studied side by side, the two letters teach us to distinguish between biblical separation and unbiblical schism.

We Must Separate from Those Who Pervert the Gospel (2 John)

Second John is one of Scripture's clearest calls to oppose doctrinal error. The apostle John wrote this little letter to command Christian churches to defend the gospel against those who twist or deny it. Doctrinal orthodoxy is essential. But mere orthodoxy isn't enough. Beyond believing and cherishing the truth, Christians must do *nothing* to aid and abet false teachers.

John may seem like an unlikely guy to talk about "the fight." He writes a great deal about love and unity—throughout the Gospel of John, over and over again in 1 John, and several more times in 2 John (vv. 1, 3, 5, 6) and 3 John (vv. 1, 6). Yes, he's the disciple whom Jesus loved (John 13:23; 20:2;

21:7, 21:20). But he's also a "son of thunder" (Mark 3:17), and he could bring the thunder when confronting false teachers.

The ease with which John can move between Christian love and Christian conflict is instructive. In one sense he reminds me of Jude. *I want to talk about the gospel,* Jude said, *but I need to talk about apostasy.* Yet, what we see in John's letters feels a bit different. He doesn't alternate between topics—sometimes talking about love and other times talking about defending the faith. No, the two motifs are intertwined. *We defend the truth because we love the truth. We cut off false teachers because we love Christ's church. We eagerly express our love—but it is love in truth (2 John 1, 6; 3 John 1).*

Once again, we see that Scripture doesn't allow us to choose between truth and love. Even if some Christians are more loving by nature and some are hardwired to defend the faith, *all* Christians are to love each other, and *all* Christians are to oppose false teaching. Love *and* truth—not love *or* truth. John Stott writes, "Our love grows soft if it is not strengthened by truth, and our truth hard if it is not softened by love. Scripture commands us both to love each other in the truth and to hold the truth in love."[94]

After John's initial greeting at the start of 2 John, the apostle warns his readers to beware of false teachers. He twice labels the heretics "deceivers," the second time adding the unambiguous descriptor "antichrist" (vv. 7–8). John uses the term "antichrist" for false teachers in 1 John as well (2:18, 22; 4:3). If it sounds like a severe description, he intends it to. The false teachers are wrong about the very core of Christianity—"the coming of Christ in the flesh" (2 John 7).

John doesn't content himself with this general warning. He insists that the church must have *nothing* to do with false teachers. And it will not do to oppose only false teaching; Scripture commands us to oppose false *teachers.* According to John, even hosting false teachers or wishing them well makes us partakers of their wickedness (vv. 10–11). If a mere greeting makes us liable for error, how much more does active cooperation with apostasy incur our guilt? Scripture teaches a legitimate "guilt by association" here and elsewhere (1 Timothy 5:22). Our alliances matter.

---

94   John R. W. Stott, *The Letters of John: An Introduction and Commentary* (Grand Rapids, MI: William B. Eerdmans Publishing Co., 1988), 207.

We must oppose false teachers. That's the message of 2 John, and for my entire ministry, I've embraced it. But we must not fall in love with conflict and start aiming our spiritual guns at faithful Christian brothers. That's the message of 3 John—a message I took much longer to learn.

We Should Cooperate with Those Who Promote the Gospel (3 John 5–8)

Third John teaches us the flipside of what we learned in 2 John—that collaboration with truth-tellers promotes the gospel. Unlike 2 John, 3 John has a specific plotline and a cast of characters, complete with a named antagonist. The story focuses on "the brothers," a group of Christians who had visited the church to which John was writing. John mentions these brothers three times (vv. 3, 5, 10), and he urges the church to help fund their ministry (vv. 5–8).

We don't know a lot about these brothers. We know they were guests— "strangers" to the church (v. 5). They weren't home-grown. They weren't insiders. Ah, but they were fellow believers. Only within the Christian faith can one be both a stranger and a brother. We also know that they were missionaries. Apparently, they had come to the church to present their upcoming missionary work: "They have gone out for the sake of the name" (v. 7). There's a missions book or two in that phrase, though this book isn't it.[95] The phrase is a beautiful, God-centered description of missions and missionaries: These brothers had left home to go abroad with the message of Jesus Christ, and their motive was the glory of Jesus' name. Awesome!

John's main goal in writing this little letter was to encourage the church to support these brothers. In fact, this is perhaps the clearest New Testament example of missionary deputation, our modern term for the often challenging process in which missionaries visit churches to raise a team of financial and prayer partners. The church in 3 John had hosted and helped these brothers. Although John had warned the church *not* to host false teachers, he commends the church for their kindness to these good brothers. *I've heard how you treated them when they were with you (v. 3). They shared that you helped them (vv. 5–6)—and I'm proud of you! Well done! Now, do more for them. Outfit them. Help them get where they're*

---

95   I'm grateful for two books that highlight a God-glorifying motive for missions: John Piper's *Let the Nations Be Glad* and Dave Doran's *For the Sake of His Name*. The latter was the inspiration for my missions hymn by the same title: churchworksmedia.com/product/for-the-sake-of-his-name-free.

going. Treat them the way you would treat the Lord if He were visiting (v. 6). They are depending on the financial support of Christians and churches—not unbelievers (v. 7). We ought to support people like this, even if they don't have previous connections to us (v. 8).

I love that. All of it!

Here's where the comparison between 2 John and 3 John gets so interesting. We've learned that if we assist false teachers in any way, we share their guilt (2 John 10–11). But the principle works positively as well! If we support gospel teachers, we share their success: we are "fellow workers for the truth" (3 John 8). Did you get that? When you support a gospel-centered ministry, God considers you to be a *partner* in that ministry. It almost sounds like a multi-level scheme. So, if your church gives financial help to a missionary in Peru, or if you spend time praying for a mission ministry in Cambodia, you're rewarded for that work—even if you've never left your hometown. How great is that?! Don't help heretics. Do help missionaries!

I appreciate the way John encourages the church to have open arms to welcome fellow believers and open wallets to assist them. Yes, there are enemies of the gospel out there. You'll recognize them easily enough. But there are also *brothers* doing good gospel work! God forbid that we should confuse the two categories. We must open our hearts to faithful men and women. They may not have grown up in our church. Perhaps they didn't attend one of our favorite colleges or seminaries. But we serve the same Savior. We share the same Father. We are indwelt by the same Spirit. They are brothers and sisters, and we should treat them that way.

Opposing a false teacher makes you a hero. But opposing a fellow believer makes you a villain. Which brings us to Diotrephes.

We Must Not Treat Brothers like Enemies (3 John 9–12)

It's a tragedy when separation turns to schism. That's the main reason why I wrote this book! I've seen it happen in church history. And I've crossed that line myself. As I mentioned earlier, it was an uncomfortable moment when I realized that much of my separatism reflected the work of Diotrephes rather than Jude. Diotrephes "earnestly contended"—but with the wrong people, over the wrong things. It's a cautionary tale we need to hear.

Let's talk about Diotrephes. Who was this guy? And what was his problem?

Well, it appears that he was a leader in the church to which John was writing. John mentions a couple other church leaders as well—Gaius in verse 1 and Demetrius in verse 12. But it seems that there was a power struggle in the church. Raise your hand if you've seen this movie before in your own church. I have, and I find some strange encouragement from the fact that even first-century churches had these issues.

Anyway, there was a conflict between Diotrephes and another church leader, Demetrius, and John clearly sides with the latter. Third John 11–12 seems to be an encouragement for the church to line up behind Demetrius.

Now, the name *Diotrephes* means "trouble-making punk" in Greek. Okay, I made that up. But Diotrephes is not a good guy. You've never met a Christian family who named their son Diotrephes. He fought *everybody*!

First, he opposed the apostle John. The guy had guts—I'll give him that. He had the audacity to oppose the *last living disciple*. John writes, "Diotrephes…does not acknowledge our authority" (v. 9). He unpacks the problem a bit, explaining that Diotrephes was "talking wicked nonsense against us" (v. 10). The Greek word translated as "wicked nonsense" is *twitter*. Okay, I made that up, too. But he'd have made good use of social media if it had been an option.

Beyond opposing John, Diotrephes opposed "the brothers." When these missionaries had visited the church, most of the members had welcomed them. But not Diotrephes! He wouldn't receive them, and he threatened the church members who *did* receive them with excommunication (v. 10). Apparently, the guy had enough influence in the church that he could coerce people into going along with his divisiveness. He moved from first-degree schism to second-degree schism. What does that mean? He cut off those who didn't cut off the brothers. Follow that? It's complicated. But again, I've lived it.

So why did Diotrephes stir up so much trouble? Perhaps he had convinced himself that he was serving the Lord, but John cuts through the clutter and exposes his true motives: "Diotrephes…likes to put himself first" (v. 9). He wanted "to have the preeminence" (KJV). Whereas the brothers went out for the sake of Jesus' name, Diotrephes labored for the sake of *his own name*. This is important. Diotrephes was separating from faithful, gospel-preaching brothers not because there was a doctrinal problem but because he was afraid they would somehow erode his own influence. It was nothing but a power play. In the words of my friend Tranwei Yu, "He isolated himself to elevate himself." Pastor John MacArthur comments, "By rejecting those who were representing Christ, Diotrephes was in effect usurping His role as the head of the church."[96] But make no mistake: Only *One* is preeminent in Jesus' church (Colossians 1:18).

Let's call it like it is. Diotrephes would rather protect his turf than see the gospel go to the unreached. He was fine with the heathen going to hell, as long as he could be the big shot at home. He opposed an apostle, fought fellow leaders, intimidated church members, and blacklisted missionaries—all to feed his own stinking pride. Disgusting.

Diotrephes didn't love others because he was too busy loving himself. Unity was a threat to his own selfish ambition, so he undermined it through bogus separation. As ironic as it sounds, the church needs to *separate* from such people.

Every Diotrephes fancies himself a Jude. Read that again. *Every Diotrephes fancies himself a Jude.* I did. There were times in my ministry when I was conscientiously trying to obey Scripture even as I critiqued faithful Christians, blogged about foolish controversies, and gloried in "red-meat" discourse. It was bad for the cause of Christ. And it was bad for me—suffocating to my very soul. Like Diotrephes, I ostracized faithful brothers, choosing instead to play to my audience and promote my own interests. My behavior was "wicked nonsense" (v. 10).

And so, it breaks my heart when I see orthodox brothers taking shots at each other. We zing our brothers from conference platforms and pulpits. We cancel each other over a judgment call we don't like. We ignore the 99% alignment we share and exaggerate the importance of the 1% where we see things differently.

I appreciate the way Conrad Mbewe sounds the same alarm:

> Too many Christians are fighting battles they have no business with, simply because they have been drawn in by their allegiance to individuals who have scores to settle with their *perceived ecclesiastical*

---

96   John MacArthur, *The MacArthur New Testament Commentary: 1–3 John* (Chicago, IL: Moody Publishers, 2007), 256.

adversaries. The animosity is veiled under the claim that an issue must be addressed or else the Christian faith will suffer a mortal wound. But anyone who compares the amount of dust being raised relative to the importance of the issue at hand soon realizes that there must be some other deep underlying issues. The heat being generated is not in proportion to the issue at hand. Often a personal grudge is driving the entire train into a gorge. It must be stopped.[97]

Yes, we need to oppose apostasy. But we need to support faithful brothers. And God help us if we've gotten so accustomed to conflict that we can't tell the difference.

---

97   Mbewe, 66.

CHAPTER 9

PETER AND
THE FEAR
OF MAN

*"But when Cephas came to Antioch, I opposed him to his face, because
he stood condemned. For before certain men came from James,
he was eating with the Gentiles; but when they came
he drew back and separated himself,
fearing the circumcision party."*

—*Galatians 2:11–12*

Courage is a beautiful thing. Admirable. Inspiring. We love stories, whether on film or in print, of those who demonstrate courage in the face of adversity.

I remember my immense enjoyment when I first read John F. Kennedy's Pulitzer-Prize-winning book *Profiles in Courage*, which he authored years before ascending to the presidency. He writes:

> This is a book about that most admirable of human virtues—courage. "Grace under pressure," Ernest Hemingway defined it. And these are the stories of the pressures experienced by eight United States Senators and the grace with which they endured them—the risks to their careers, the unpopularity of their courses, the defamation of their characters, and sometimes, but sadly only sometimes, the vindication of their reputations and their principles.[98]

---

98   John F. Kennedy, *Profiles in Courage* (New York, NY: HarperCollins, 2003), 1.

Like Kennedy, I love the idea of leaders who do what's right even when it's not popular. May God grant us more men and women with such poll-spurning conviction!

Scripture and church history are filled with people who demonstrated courage in the face of adversity. A Moses. A Joseph. A Daniel. A Shadrach, a Meshach, and an Abednego. An Esther. A Paul, who reminded Timothy, "God has not given us a spirit of fear" (2 Timothy 1:7 NKJV). A Luther, who faced a room full of opponents and a world full of devils and still cried out, "Here I stand. I can do no other." A John Knox, whose eulogy by Regen Morton included an unforgettably inspiring line: "Here lies one who neither flattered nor feared any flesh."[99]

In this chapter we consider Peter. Brash Peter. Impulsive Peter. Outspoken Peter. Courageous Peter, in the early chapters of Acts. But here, in Galatians 2, cowardly Peter.

I'll admit that calling Peter cowardly is a bit severe. First, I like the guy. I relate to him—I've heard that it's possible to have an opinion without sharing it, but I've seldom tried. Peter wasn't generally timid. There were times when he was shockingly audacious, like when he rebuked Jesus for talking about the cross (Matthew 16:21–23). (Aside: Having the Son of God call you "Satan" has to leave a mark.) On the night of Jesus' arrest, Peter oscillated between the foolhardy courage that cut off Malchus' ear and the self-protective fear that denied Jesus three times (John 18:10; Matthew 26:69–75). Of course, Jesus' resurrection and the outpouring of the Spirit put steel into Peter's spine; he preached with boldness and defied the Sanhedrin in Acts 2–4.

But in the event that Paul recounts in Galatians 2, the pendulum swung back toward cowardice. Paul rehearses a time when Cephas (a.k.a., Peter) failed so miserably that Paul had to confront him "to his face." I hope there's a VHS recording of the event somewhere in heaven. This is a big deal: the New Testament's two champions squaring off. This is Ali vs. Frazier. Not Batman vs. Joker (which we might expect), but Batman vs. Superman. This is *big*—a momentous confrontation that likely caused the Earth to move just a bit. The late pastor and theologian John Stott writes, "This is without doubt one of the most tense and dramatic episodes of the

---

99   Edward M. Panosian, "John Knox: The Thundering Scot" in *Faith of Our Fathers: Scenes from Church History*, ed. Mark Sidwell (Greenville, SC: Bob Jones University Press, 1989), 112.

New Testament. Here are two leading apostles of Jesus Christ face to face in complete and open conflict."[100]

Pay close attention to Galatians 2:11–14:

> But when Cephas came to Antioch, I opposed him to his face, because he stood condemned. For before certain men came from James, he was eating with the Gentiles; but when they came he drew back and separated himself, fearing the circumcision party. And the rest of the Jews acted hypocritically along with him, so that even Barnabas was led astray by their hypocrisy. But when I saw that their conduct was not in step with the truth of the gospel, I said to Cephas before them all, "If you, though a Jew, live like a Gentile and not like a Jew, how can you force the Gentiles to live like Jews?"

Illegitimate Separation Warrants a Stern Rebuke

What had Peter done wrong? At first glance, not a lot. He had eaten with Gentile Christians—and then he had stopped eating with Gentile Christians. It seems relatively harmless, if a bit rude.

But more than a meal was at stake. This wasn't just a junior high popularity contest that determined who could sit at the cool kids' table. The very purity of the gospel was at stake. When Peter "separated himself" from the Gentile believers, he was siding with the legalists. It wasn't about lunch; it was about Christian fellowship. It was about access to the gospel—and even about the nature of the gospel itself. Paul blames Peter for *confusing the gospel by his illegitimate separation*—a separation motivated by fear.[101]

Let's take a look at the backstory. What's going on? Well, there was a debate regarding the acceptance of Gentiles into the church—a debate that would eventually be settled in the Jerusalem council, which very likely took place *after* the writing of Galatians. (I can't be dogmatic here, but I wouldn't expect Peter to contradict the council if it had happened beforehand, nor can I imagine Paul not citing the council in Galatians.) The gist of the

---

100   John R. Stott, *The Message of Galatians: Only One Way* (Downers Grove, IL: IVP Academic, 1968), 49.

101   The term "drew back" in Galatians 2:12 is the same word Paul uses in Acts 20:20 and 27, when he says he didn't shrink back in fear from preaching the Scriptures to the Ephesians. J. B. Lightfoot comments, "The words describe forcibly the cautious withdrawal of a timid person who shrinks from observation." *St. Paul's Epistle to the Galatians* (Peabody, MA: Hendrickson Publishers, 1993), 112.

conflict was this: *Could Gentiles come directly to Christ and be saved, or did they also need to adopt some Jewish traditions, such as circumcision?* The stakes were high. Are people saved by faith-plus or by faith-alone? In response, Paul wrote Galatians—a letter that defends the purity of the gospel while simultaneously denouncing those who preach another gospel (Galatians 1:8–9; 5:12).

So, what did Peter do wrong? Well, Peter knew that Gentiles should be welcomed into the body of Christ as equals with Jews. He had watched Jesus serve Gentiles throughout His three-year ministry, from a centurion to a Samaritan woman to an entire Samaritan village. He had heard Jesus give repeated commands to witness, preach, and make disciples *everywhere* (Matthew 28:18–20; Mark 16:15; Luke 24:46–48; Acts 1:8). Most significantly, he had been commanded by the ascended Lord three times to overcome his own prejudice by (a) eating previously unclean foods in order to teach him to (b) evangelize previously unclean people, the Gentiles (Acts 10). When he did finally go to Caesarea and preach, Cornelius and his household came to Jesus before Peter even finished his sermon. Of all people, Peter understood that Gentiles were accepted into the Christian household on equal footing with Jews.

Ironically, Peter specifically told the Gentiles in Caesarea—and the Judaizers in Jerusalem!—that God had revealed to him the necessity of receiving Gentile believers as brothers:

> And he said to them, "You yourselves [Gentiles] know how unlawful it is for a Jew to associate with or to visit anyone of another nation, but God has shown me that I should not call any person common or unclean." (Acts 10:28)

> So Peter opened his mouth [to Cornelius and other Gentiles] and said: "Truly I understand that God shows no partiality, but in every nation anyone who fears him and does what is right is acceptable to him." (Acts 10:34–35)

> So when Peter went up to Jerusalem, the circumcision party criticized him, saying, "You went to uncircumcised men and ate with them." But Peter began and explained it to them in order. (Acts 11:3–4)

Shortly after Peter's ministry in Caesarea, the gospel began to get *real* traction among Gentiles. When the gospel advanced to the city of Antioch, unnamed Christians decided to stop targeting only fellow Jews with the gospel. *Here's a thought: Let's just give the gospel to everybody—Jew or Gentile, monotheist or pagan polytheist. If you're human, we'll tell you about Jesus.* They did, God smiled on their efforts, and the powerhouse church at Antioch was born (Acts 11:19–21).

Barnabas was sent from Jerusalem to be the founding pastor of the Antioch church, and he eventually retrieved Saul from Tarsus to be his "youth pastor" (Acts 11:22–26). And at some point that the book of Acts doesn't record, Peter visited the church. He connected with the formerly pagan believers. Despite the prejudice that previously had kept Jews from eating with Gentiles, Peter shared a meal with these new believers, fellowshipped with them, and affirmed their gospel identity. Based on what we read above from Acts 10–11, he got it. He had learned the lesson in Caesarea and acted on it in Antioch. So long as embracing Gentile brothers was the popular thing to do, that is.

Illegitimate Separation Often Stems from the Fear of Man

But then more Jews from Jerusalem came to Antioch. These men were sent by James, and they likely were faithful Christians. But their arrival somehow brought with it concerns about the "circumcision party"—likely Judaizers (Galatians 2:11).[102] These people expected Gentile believers to adopt Judaism en route to Christianity. Faced with a raised eyebrow and the potential of a scandal among the Jews, Peter folded like a deck of cards. He went along with the Jews' narrow exclusivity like he was suddenly offended by Gentile believers. "What happens in Antioch stays in Antioch." Even Barnabas—the pastor of the Antioch church!—followed Peter's hypocrisy for a time (Galatians 2:13). Peter and Barnabas held the Gentiles at arms' length, at least while the Judaizers were in town. In the words of Galatians 2:12, Peter "separated himself"—not out of principle, but out of fear of legalistic Jews.

Here's the thing: Illegitimate separation isn't harmless. It hurts people. It hinders the cause of Christ. It even clouds the purity of the gospel. By eating with Gentiles, Peter was actually treating them as equals—and

---

102   D. A. Carson provides a lengthy discussion on the "men from James" and the "circumcision party" in *Love in Hard Places* (Wheaton, IL: Crossway Books, 2002), 150–62.

thereby affirming the gospel that saved them. But by avoiding Gentiles, Peter actually undermined the gospel. Why? Because he treated legitimate brothers in Christ as though they were outside the fellowship.

Paul wouldn't have it. He didn't care that Peter was a central figure in the New Testament church, nor that Barnabas was a close friend and mentor. He had already said that even a false-teaching *angel* should be accursed (Galatians 1:8). Paul was bound to defend the purity of the Christian gospel regardless of who opposed or confused it. When Peter made a grave error and "stood condemned," Paul called him out for his fear of man and his hypocrisy. What's more, he rebuked Peter in public since the error had been public.

Illegitimate Separation Obscures the Gospel

Notice that Paul specifically says that the behavior of Peter and Barnabas "was not in step with the truth of the gospel" (Galatians 2:14). That's a serious charge. They thought they were just avoiding unnecessary controversy with their more conservative friends. Maybe they congratulated themselves on the peacekeeping nature of their decision. *But their decision to cut off faithful brothers from normal fellowship was out of step with the gospel.* Paul courageously told them so, both through an in-person rebuke and by including the event in the holy Scriptures. In so doing, Paul essentially modeled the kind of Christian restoration he commands in Galatians 6:1. It also says much about Peter's humility that he apparently accepted the rebuke and was restored along with Barnabas. As proof, Peter speaks warmly of Paul as his "dear brother" in 2 Peter 3:15, years later.

Ironically, I've heard Galatians 2 preached in defense of separation from fellow Christians based on Paul's confrontation of Peter. But the passage actually teaches the exact opposite. Rather than focusing on Paul's rebuke of Peter, we should focus on *why* Paul rebuked Peter. The answer is that *Paul rebuked Peter for undermining the gospel through illegitimate separation.*

Now, remember Part 2 of this book—that separation from false teachers and unrepentant Christians is essential. I'm a separatist. But separation is legitimate only when Scripture commands it. Contrary to what I've heard from other separatists over the years, it is indeed possible to be "too separated." It's essential that we see the difference between legitimate and illegitimate separation.

Legitimate separation protects the gospel. It is motivated by a love of the gospel. It defends the truth.

Illegitimate separation undermines the gospel. It is motivated by the fear of man. It defends turf—whether that means a power structure, personal prestige, or man-made addendums to Scripture.

Let's draw this chapter to a close by making applications to the twenty-first-century church.

First, I get Peter. I understand Barnabas. I too have been intimidated into breaking fellowship with orthodox Christian brothers and sisters because I feared the poor opinion of my most conservative friends. I understand the snare of the fear of man!

There were times when I exercised a schismatic spirit with a clear conscience, sincerely believing I was doing what Scripture required. But there were also times when I just toed the party line to avoid criticism. I'm ashamed of that now, but I do understand it. If that's you—if you're making decisions regarding fellowship and separation based on others' opinions rather than clear biblical principles, check yourself. Repent of your cowardice and the schism it has fostered. And by God's grace, change.

I never meant to hurt anybody, much less confuse the gospel. Peter and Barnabas didn't either. They likely didn't actually *teach* legalism. They just tolerated it. But their actions had serious implications. Derek Thomas explains:

> Neither Peter nor Barnabas were denying the gospel verbally. But their actions were calling it into question. By their inconsistency, by going back on what they had already practiced before this time, they were undoing the validity of their own testimony and wounding the understanding of others as to the nature of the gospel.[103]

Christian unity is so important. It is *produced* by the gospel. But it also *displays* the gospel. May God help us to preserve it—even if doing so earns us some raised eyebrows.

---

103 Derek Thomas, *Let's Study Galatians* (Carlisle, PA: Banner of Truth Trust, 2004), 53.

CHAPTER 10

THE HOLY CORINTHIAN MESS

"I appeal to you, brothers, by the name of our Lord Jesus Christ,
that all of you agree, and that there be no divisions among you,
but that you be united in the same mind
and the same judgment."

—*1 Corinthians 1:10*

Imagine that a long-time friend calls you, seeking your advice. Through tears, she tells you that her church is in crisis. There are factions—some supporting one pastor, some supporting another. A deacon is suing another deacon over a business deal gone wrong. One of the wealthiest members— a generous giver—is involved in an incestuous relationship, but nobody is willing to confront him. People are actually getting drunk at church events. The church is a hot mess.

Would you tell her to leave the church? Find a new one? I would!

Of course, what I've described isn't fiction. With slight adjustments, each of those scenarios comes from the book of 1 Corinthians and describes the mess going on in Corinth. And yet Paul, writing to "the saints at Corinth" (1 Corinthians 1:1), didn't tell them to pack it in or close up shop. He told them to get their act together—to repent.

Now, I know the illustration is flawed. There was very likely no other Christian church in Corinth. There wasn't another option. Plus, modern churches have 2,000 years of church history—and a completed canon of Scripture—telling us what a healthy church looks like. We have more information and more responsibility. Your friend should probably find another church if there is a better option. I'm not an idiot.

But I do believe this: We are far too comfortable criticizing churches and far too cavalier about writing off churches, whether our own or the church down the street. In some circles, it's actually a mark of spiritual discernment to uncork on the "compromising" church across town, even if it's a gospel-preaching church. Our willingness to badmouth our brothers and sisters is a scandal. We're guilty of schism.

I'll never forget witnessing an example of this nearly two decades ago. The church I pastored had a makeshift "float" in a community parade. We wore t-shirts to identify ourselves and distributed literature to invite people to visit our services. Another church—a more contemporary church—was doing the same thing, but their float was a stage for their praise band. Their music had a serious "thump" to it. Our churches had some notable differences, but both preached the gospel. And so, I was heartsick to see the disgust—I might even say the *hatred*—on the face of one of our church members as he glared at them across the parking lot. It seemed like he wanted to call down fire from heaven, a la Luke 9:54. Is such antipathy justified? Are we authorized to censure a gospel-preaching church if it's really flawed, or if it uses music we don't like? First Corinthians has a lot to say about this if we're willing to listen. I'll focus our attention on portions of chapters 1, 3, and 12.

Even Flawed Churches Are Home to God's People (1:1–9)

Paul almost seems schizophrenic in the book of 1 Corinthians. Throughout the book he absolutely unleashes on the church for its overt carnality (3:1, 3). Everything that could go wrong did go wrong in the Corinth church, it seems. Divisiveness (chs. 1–4). Moral scandals (ch. 5). Lawsuits (ch. 6). Favoritism, neglect of the poor, and drunkenness (ch. 11). The abuse of the gift of tongues (chs. 12–14). The denial of a key doctrine (ch. 15). *What. A. Mess.* D. A. Carson calls the Corinthian church "wretchedly immature believers...who are acting like pagans."[104] I've driven by a number of

---

104   D. A. Carson, *The Cross and Christian Ministry: Leadership Lessons from 1 Corinthians* (Grand Rapids, MI: Baker Books, 1993), 72–73.

churches in my lifetime that were called "Corinth Baptist Church," and each time I scratched my head a bit, though I admired their honesty.

And yet Paul writes to the Corinthian Christians with deep affection. More than that, he writes to them with deep admiration. Look at his first nine verses to them:

> Paul, called by the will of God to be an apostle of Christ Jesus, and our brother Sosthenes, to the church of God that is in Corinth, to those sanctified in Christ Jesus, called to be saints together with all those who in every place call upon the name of our Lord Jesus Christ, both their Lord and ours: Grace to you and peace from God our Father and the Lord Jesus Christ. I give thanks to my God always for you because of the grace of God that was given you in Christ Jesus, that in every way you were enriched in him in all speech and all knowledge—even as the testimony about Christ was confirmed among you—so that you are not lacking in any gift, as you wait for the revealing of our Lord Jesus Christ, who will sustain you to the end, guiltless in the day of our Lord Jesus Christ. God is faithful, by whom you were called into the fellowship of his Son, Jesus Christ our Lord. (1 Corinthians 1:1–9)

Maybe you're nodding, knowingly: "He's just buttering them up before laying them out." But no, that's not it. Paul didn't have an insincere bone in his body. He loved these people. He had spent eighteen months with them—likely as long as he spent in any single church other than Ephesus, where he spent three years. Whereas we read the book and only see the scandals, Paul was writing to *people*—many of whom he had likely led to the Lord. This carnal church was one he started. These rebellious people were his children in the faith.

But even that doesn't account for the introduction to the letter. Paul isn't just being nice to people he loved, in spite of themselves. He writes to them about the work God had done in their lives. They had a spiritual pulse and a Christian legacy. He legitimately thanks God for their faith in Christ. Let's lean into his description of the Corinthian believers.

First, notice how he addresses them:

> You are a *church* (v. 2). You are *sanctified* in Christ Jesus (v. 2). You are called to be *saints*—just like everyone else who knows Jesus (v. 2). You are *subjects* of the Lord (v. 2). You are recipients of *grace* and *peace*

from God (v. 3). You are *children* of God our Father (v. 3). You are a cause of my *thanksgiving* (v. 4). You are spiritually *rich* in Christ Jesus (v. 5). You are *knowledgeable* and *gifted* (vv. 5–7). You are awaiting the return of Jesus—and *He will sustain you* to the end (vv. 7–8). You are in process, and you will one day be *guiltless* (v. 8). You were *called* by our faithful God, and you have *fellowship with His Son* (v. 9).

That's a lot! My first thought is that maybe he copied and pasted a greeting intended for the Thessalonians. To Paul, this shabby group of Christians was deserving of honor. They were the recipients of God's soul-saving grace. Jesus wasn't done with them yet, so neither was Paul. Jesus would keep them until the end and finish in them the work He had begun. They were worth fighting for. We can learn something from all of that! For starters, we can thank God for what He is doing in that "squishy" evangelical church around the corner, and we can pray for their progress in godliness, confident that God will win out in the end.

Now, perhaps most notable is the fact that Paul twice refers to these Corinthians as holy—"sanctified" and "saints" (v. 2). He speaks not of their conduct (clearly!), but of their spiritual standing. On second thought, "spiritual standing" is an insufficient description. That's the language of justification, where Christians are declared to be righteous in spite of our sin. That's glorious—but this is even more.

Holiness in Christ wasn't just the standing or position of the Corinthians. It was their new *identity* and new *reality*. Joined to Christ, they *were* holy. They had been definitively *set apart from sin*; its power over them was officially broken. This wasn't just a forensic ideal, as with justification, but an actual change in their relationships with God and with sin. They were now new people who were deeply united to God and radically severed from sin. And as a result of that definitive and very real sanctification, they needed to become holy in their conduct—"to live up to who they are," in theologian Thomas Schreiner's words.[105] Their definitive sanctification needed to trickle down into their progressive sanctification.

Paul's commendations aren't focused only on what Christ had done for these people, though there's an unmistakable emphasis on grace. He also

---

105   Thomas R. Schreiner, *1 Corinthians* (Downers Grove, IL: IVP Academic, 2018), 51. Notice that Schreiner doesn't say they should live up to their position, but "live up to who they *are*." I'm grateful to Dr. Mark Snoeberger for sharpening my understanding of definitive sanctification.

speaks of their testimony, their giftedness, their longing for Jesus' return. He genuinely admires these people for their imperfect but sincere love for Jesus.

I contrast Paul's attitude toward these people with my own, and I wonder what the book of 1 Corinthians would look like if I had written it twenty years ago. It would likely be short and sweet (though those I've pastored will likely balk at "short"). I'll take a stab at it.

Dear Corinthians,

You're an absolute disaster. I don't even know where to begin. But there's too much wrong here. The few godly people there should find a new church. The rest of you should stop playing games and decide if you really want to pursue Christ. But if we're doing this, we're starting over. Let's kill the church and plant another under a new name.

I'm kind of kidding. But such thinking reflects too low a view of Jesus' church. This band of remarkably worldly Christians was "the church of God at Corinth" (1:2). God wasn't ashamed to claim them. Nor was Paul.

Even Flawed Churches Are Home to God's Spirit (3:16–17)

We move now to chapter 3 of 1 Corinthians. In 1 Corinthians 3:1–4, Paul calls the Corinthian church spiritual infants who are both carnal and "merely human"—despite the fact that they are Christian "brothers" (v. 1). None of that is surprising. What is surprising is that in 1 Corinthians 3:16 Paul refers to the church collectively as the Temple of God. The fact that God's holy people call Bible-teaching churches "home" is one thing. But the fact that God's Holy Spirit calls a church as shabby as the one in Corinth His "home"—His dwelling place—is remarkable. In the Old Testament, God uniquely resided in the Tabernacle and Temple. But since Pentecost, God has lived within His people as His living Temple (1 Peter 2:5). Even the miraculous symbol in the upper room in Acts 2—tongues of fire hovering above believers—highlights the fact that God's new residence is His people, not a building.[106]

---

106   See my article "Pentecost & Missions" in *Gospel Meditations for Missions* (Church Works Media, 2011), Day 16.

God lives in individual Christians as well. That's the point of Paul's urging the Corinthian believers to purity in 1 Corinthians 6:19–20. There, he tells individual believers, "Your body is a temple of the Holy Spirit within you." But in chapter 3, Paul is addressing the entire church. He's been using the building analogy throughout the chapter, noting that various leaders are not rivals but fellow-builders of God's Temple in the city of Corinth: the church. That's why the pronouns in 3:16–17 are plural in the original Greek: "you [plural, as a group] are God's Temple".... "God's Spirit dwells in you [plural, as a group]".... "God's temple is holy, and you [plural, as a group] are that temple." Bottom line: The church—even a church with as many problems as the church at Corinth—is God's Temple.

What difference does that make? Keep reading.

First Corinthians 3:16 is inspiring. But 1 Corinthians 3:17 is frightening. It says that God will "destroy" those who destroy His Temple. Here's the imagery: Think of how protective God was of the Old Testament Temple. Only believers could enter—and only after going through symbolic purifications and sacrifices. Only priests could access the Holy Place. Beyond that, only the *high priest* could access the Holy of Holies—and that only once per year, on the Day of Atonement. When people defiled the Temple, they died. Think of Hophni and Phineas (1 Samuel 2:12–17, 22–26, 34; 4:11). The Temple was so sacred that even construction noises were avoided during its construction (1 Kings 6:7). With all of that in mind, can you imagine rushing into God's Temple and defacing it, say, through graffiti or vandalism? Only if you had a death wish!

But Paul says that those who harm the local church are actually defacing God's Temple. And God will destroy them! This is vitally important. The whole point of chapter 3 is to reprove division in the church. Paul took them to task for their sectarian spirit: "For when one says, 'I follow Paul,' and another, 'I follow Apollos,' are you not being merely human?" (v. 4).

Paul argues for unity from a variety of angles, but his climactic argument is that the church—even a church as messed up as Corinth—is God's Temple. And that's not just a theoretical concept. It has teeth. If you keep defacing the church—through criticism, infighting, rivalry, gossip, and so on—God will judge you.[107]

---

107   Kistemaker writes, "The behavior—strife, jealousy, immorality, and permissiveness—of the Christians in Corinth was reprehensible. By their conduct the Corinthians were desecrating God's

What does that mean to us today? We should value every gospel-preaching church, imperfect as it may be. And more to the point, we should fear raising a finger—or a voice—against any body of believers. Yes, we need to exercise discernment. But to *attack* Christ's church is dangerous. D. A. Carson writes that the main point of 1 Corinthians 3 is that "God loves the church and jealously guards it as the dwelling place of his own Spirit."[108] Even a church like the one in Corinth. We might well repurpose 1 Chronicles 16:22 to refer to the church: "Touch not God's anointed." To put it bluntly: *Don't mess with Christ's church!*

Even Flawed Churches Are Worth Saving (1 Corinthians 12)

We've cherry-picked our way through 1 Corinthians. But I hope the message is connecting. Deriding God's church is no way to curry God's favor. We should put a hand over our mouths when we're tempted to speak a critical word about God's people.

I'd like to close this chapter with a very inadequate look at 1 Corinthians 12. Here, Paul uses the imagery of a human body as a picture of the church. The New Testament uses a variety of images as illustrations of the church, but the body image is the most common, and perhaps the most profound. With relentless attention throughout the chapter, Paul keeps reminding the carnal Corinthian Christians that *they are members of the same church body* (12:12, 13, 14, 15, 16, 17, 18, 19, 20, 22, 24, 27). He makes a similar argument in Romans 12, but not as thoroughly as he does here.

The placement of this imagery in the book of 1 Corinthians is important. Paul didn't tell the believers there to get out while they could. He didn't suggest their departure from that church—not even once. Rather, he reminded them that their unity is rooted in the very gospel and in the unifying work of the Holy Spirit: "For in one Spirit we were all baptized into one body—Jews or Greeks, slaves or free—and all were made to drink of one Spirit" (12:13). As messed up as they were, Paul kept *pushing them together*.[109]

---

temple." Simon J. Kistemaker, *New Testament Commentary: Exposition of the First Epistle to the Corinthians* (Grand Rapids, MI: Baker Academic, 1993), 117.

108   Carson, *The Cross*, 83.

109   Ernest Pickering makes a fair counterpoint when he points out that the Corinthian errors "were

Did it work? Well, the book of 2 Corinthians indicates that Paul's concerns about this particular assembly weren't over. But it also shows progress. One whom they had disciplined out of the church—I assume the incestuous man from 1 Corinthians 5—had been rescued. He had repented, and Paul urged the church to receive him (2 Corinthians 2:5–11). We can rejoice at the sinner's return. But we can also rejoice that a church that had callously tolerated gross immorality had heeded Paul's command and exercised church discipline. And the fact that they appeared to be reluctant to readmit the repentant sinner to their fellowship indicates that they were now taking the church's purity seriously. Progress!

The rest of 2 Corinthians addresses more problems. But it also discusses opportunities. The Corinthian Christians are called "new creatures" (5:17). They are called "Christ's ambassadors" who have been entrusted with the message of the gospel (5:18–20). They are the recipients of one of Paul's most beautiful encapsulations of the gospel (5:21). They are invited to give generously to advance Paul's ministry (chs. 8–9). They are given a detailed defense of Paul's apostleship (chs. 10–11). In other words, they continued doing life and ministry together. And Paul's signoff at the end of the book is full of hope:

> Finally, brothers, rejoice. Aim for restoration, comfort one another, agree with one another, live in peace; and the God of love and peace will be with you. Greet one another with a holy kiss. All the saints greet you. The grace of the Lord Jesus Christ and the love of God and the fellowship of the Holy Spirit be with you all. (13:11–14)

One of my favorite book titles from the last twenty years is *Church Planting Is for Wimps* by Mike McKinley. The tongue-in-cheek title sets up a book about church revitalization. Any sissy can plant a church, the book says; it takes a real man to resuscitate a mostly dead church. Despite my years as a church planter, I get that. Building a new home is usually more straightforward than remodeling a money pit.

Well, Paul was no wimp. He planted the church at Corinth. But he also revitalized it. He didn't give up on it, just as Jesus didn't give up on the flawed

---

almost altogether interpersonal and moral in nature"—not doctrinal. *Biblical Separation*, 194–95. His qualification "almost" leaves room for the doctrinal errors addressed in 1 Corinthians 15, although the denial of the resurrection was far from insignificant. It is, after all, a central component of the gospel (vv. 3–4). Pickering's primary point is that we must be careful using 1 Corinthians as a blanket argument against separation, and I generally agree.

churches of Revelation 2–3. Jesus *critiqued* them. Where appropriate, he *commended* them. And at times He *warned* them that He might remove their candle and shut them down for good—a prerogative that belongs to Him, not us. But Jesus was remarkably patient with His beloved churches, and He is remarkably patient with you and me.

So, let's take a page from Paul's playbook—and from Jesus'. Let's be respectful and protective of gospel-preaching churches…flawed as they may be. Let's be patient as churches and pastors grow in grace. There may be times to lovingly point out areas where a church can improve, especially if it's a church in which we have direct responsibilities and close relationships. But don't *cancel* them. After all, to mistreat Jesus' church is to mistreat Him (Acts 9:4; 22:7; 26:14). "Touch not God's anointed."

CHAPTER 11

WORSHIP IS
NOT A
WAR

"Clap your hands, all peoples! Shout to God with loud songs of joy!
For the LORD, the Most High, is to be feared,
a great king over all the earth."

—Psalm 47:1–2

One of the most divisive issues in my Christian life has been the topic of Christian music. That's a tragedy, when you think about it. An activity that should focus exclusively on God and that should unite His people in "hymns of grateful praise" has instead become the source of contention and schism. What a shame. If the word *worship* feels like a call to arms rather than a call to prayer, we're doing it wrong.

I've been on both sides of the worship wars. I've been extremely conservative. The Amish may very well have been to my left. At a certain point in my young adult life, I was taught an exceptionally narrow view of worship music. *Exceptionally.* One example: Steve Green was way out of bounds. Another example? My wife had a recording of Michael Card lullabies that she wanted to play for our baby girls, and I made her throw it away.

On the other hand, I've recently been on the other side of the fray. As I've relaxed a bit regarding acceptable music styles, and especially as Church Works Media has published more expressive versions of our hymns, my inbox has had a bit of a target on it. I get it. I've been there.

My extreme conservatism about Christian music caused quite a bit of schism. And I blame myself. Sure, I was the product of my training. But at the end of the day, I don't blame my teachers, my environment, or my CD player. I was an adult. I was a teacher. And so, my ascetic approach to worship music was *on me*. I was mistaken—in my spirit, if not in my opinion—and I want to offer a hand to those who are dealing with similar issues.

Let's begin with where I went wrong. As I reflect on my hyper-conservatism, I believe that I arrived at certain conclusions long before I really studied the biblical data. That's a bad place to be, as Sherlock Holmes warns us: "It is a capital mistake to theorize before one has data. Insensibly one begins to twist facts to suit theories, instead of theories to suit facts."[110] A favorite piece of pastor humor is to say, "I've got a great sermon—now I just need to find a Bible verse to support it." That was me.

Despite my claim to be a strict biblicist, I *supplemented* Scripture, *twisted* Scripture, and even *contradicted* Scripture to arrive at my predetermined conclusions regarding worship music.

I Supplemented the Bible to Support My Music Standards

I've heard some fascinating extrabiblical arguments in favor of conservative music over the years. Sometimes they've been ludicrous. *Rock music kills plants.* Or, *rock music has satanic messages when played backwards.* Sometimes they've been borderline racist. *Rock music is jungle music.* Or, *converted cannibals said that CCM sounds like the music they used to worship the devil.* Sometimes the reasoning has been comically pseudo-scientific. *Rock music mixes up the alpha waves in the brain.* Or, *rock music weakens muscles.* Or, *rock music competes with the heart's natural rhythm.* Of course, sometimes arguments have been much more sophisticated. *The height of musical expression was in the Baroque period.* Or, *pop culture is unworthy of God.* The latter arguments are much more intellectually rigorous and honest, though they are still just opinions, and they feel alarmingly elitist.

I've heard respected pastors with doctoral-level educations confess that they didn't have the expertise to explain how principles of aesthetics and musicology relate to worship music. As a result, they were content to rely on "the experts." And I've heard proponents of conservative music come

---

110   Sir Arthur Conan Doyle, *A Scandal in Bohemia.*

right out and say that those who haven't studied classical music and culture as deeply as they have just aren't equipped to understand the issues in play when it comes to selecting songs and music styles for their churches. So much for the clarity of Scripture—much less its sufficiency. So much for the priesthood of the believer.

Now, I understand that there is truth outside of Scripture. We can learn much from extrabiblical sources, including on the topic of music. As both a Christian and a hymnwriter, I'm deeply indebted to skillful musicians. We should be grateful for specialists who devote their lives to important fields of study like music.

But here's the thing: We're talking about *worship*. Does an educated pastor with a completed canon and the indwelling Holy Spirit *really* lack the information to make discerning decisions about how God is to be worshiped in the church? I mentioned in this book already that our doctrinal statements usually include something about the Bible being "our only rule of faith and practice." No, the Bible doesn't tell us about performing a successful appendectomy or training for a marathon. But if anything fits within the categories of "faith and practice," it's worship! Again, I get that the doctrine of the sufficiency of Scripture doesn't mean that the Bible contains all the information we need to live on planet Earth. When I need a plumber or a lawyer, I expect that they'll have adequate training outside of the Old and New Testaments. But if the Bible isn't sufficient to instruct us on *how to please the Lord through praise*, what is it sufficient for?

One of my mentors, Dr. Michael Barrett, urges believers not to turn from Scripture to other sources when making decisions about worship.

> Advocates of contemporary methods charge traditionalists with dead formalism, and traditionalists accuse those who use modern methods with appealing to the flesh. Unhappily, the whole controversy about worship style has degenerated into arguments based on personal preference. Far too frequently, advocates on both sides, while giving verbal testimony to their concern for God's glory, defend their positions with man-centered reasoning.[111]

---

111   Michael P. V. Barrett, *The Beauty of Holiness: A Guide to Biblical Worship* (Greenville, SC: Ambassador International, 2006), 1.

The criterion for conducting or evaluating worship cannot be in terms of tradition. I know this is going to sound simplistically pious, but the only legitimate criterion for evaluating and determining worship is the Scripture, our only rule for faith and practice. If being biblical is the standard of worship, then there may even be cherished aspects of traditional worship that have to be adjusted or abandoned. Being biblical means having the resolve to either change or not change depending on what the Bible says.[112]

In hindsight, I realize I had sacrificed the doctrine of the sufficiency of Scripture to reach my desired conclusions on music. No more. Today, I encourage believers to channel the conviction of Martin Luther: "Unless I am refuted and convicted by testimonies of the Scriptures or by clear arguments...I am conquered by the Holy Scriptures.... My conscience is bound to the Word of God."[113]

I Twisted the Bible to Support My Music Standards

Some will say, "The messages I've heard in favor of conservative music *do* come from Scripture." Perhaps. But the fact that someone is using Scripture doesn't necessarily mean that the message is scriptural. What I mean is this: We must always come to the Bible to find *the author's intended meaning,* which we determine through sound interpretation—the literal, historical, grammatical hermeneutic. And yet, I've heard and preached sermons on music from passages that had nothing at all to do with music. Often— *often!*—historical narratives are used as backdrops to teach musical principles, and the result generally lands somewhere between allegorizing and begging the question. Here are some examples, along with my pushback.

Moses and Joshua confused the sound of war and the sound of music during the golden calf incident (Exodus 32:17–20). *That was a terrible event, but what does it have to do with Christian music?* Well, the idolatry was accompanied by loud music—music that sounded like a war from far away. *Again, that was a terrible event, but what does it have to do with Christian music?* Well, rock music sounds like a war. *But you're making a*

---

112   Ibid., 178.

113   Philip Schaff, *History of the Christian Church* (Grand Rapids, MI: Wm. B. Eerdmans Publishing Company, 1910), 7:304.

subjective point with no real textual backing. Are you saying Aaron invented rock music 3,400 years before Elvis? I'm saying that wrong music accompanies idolatry. *But you don't know what the music sounded like. And you could just as easily argue against Christians owning gold because gold was used to make the idols. It's all surmising.*

Uzzah was killed for touching the ark (2 Samuel 6:3–7). *Yes, but what does it have to do with Christian music?* Well, the ark was placed on an ox cart rather than being carried on staves as God commanded. *Yes, but what does it have to do with music?* Well, the Jews had learned to carry the ark on a cart from the Philistines. *Yes, but…?* Well, the Jews were trying to do God's work in the world's way, and it cost Uzzah his life, despite his good intentions. *Yes, but…?* Well, the ark is analogous to Christian lyrics and the cart is analogous to worldly music. We can't put the two together, lest we invite God's wrath. Like Uzzah did. Follow? *Actually, I don't. You're inserting music into a text that has nothing to do with music. And frankly, if you want to use the ark of the covenant to make a point about music, it would make more sense to cite David's dancing before the Lord with all his might when the ark finally entered Jerusalem, just a few verses later (2 Samuel 6:14). Follow?*

Jeroboam set up a false worship system in northern Israel to keep his people from going down to Jerusalem to worship. *Yes, but what does that have to do with music?* CCM is a false worship system, just like Jeroboam's temple. *That's an incredible leap in logic; how do you figure?* CCM uses the world's music to do God's work. *Well, that's a strong but fairly unsubstantiated opinion. And comparing CCM to Jeroboam's blatant idolatry is slanderous. If you want to compare a modern-day worship scenario to Jeroboam's idolatry—which isn't a great idea, by the way—choose actual idolatry, like Mormonism.*

You get the idea. My point is, the fact that a sermon begins with a biblical text doesn't guarantee that the arguments being made are actually biblical. I've made some of the arguments above in the past. Or I've used passages like Romans 12:1–2 and 1 John 2:15 to argue against worldliness (an accurate application). But I too often applied the concept of *worldliness* to Christian music arbitrarily and very specifically, with no real evidence. "Rock music is worldly, but classical music is godly." *Umm, how? Prove it. From Scripture.* At the time, I didn't even know that I was mishandling

Bible texts, that I was applying poor methods of Bible interpretation, or that I was making completely unsubstantiated arguments and applications.

One of the most disappointing things I've witnessed from many who argue for conservative music styles is the shockingly poor exegesis and the absolute abandonment of the text when it comes time to springboard into applications. I have seen even preachers who are well-known for sound Bible exposition radically depart from the text, making extrabiblical arguments and, sadly, pressing on people's consciences things about which Scripture is silent.[114] In many cases, I suspect that the turn away from Scripture is unintentional; I marvel at how easily I used to slip into this kind of extrabiblical argumentation myself. But I can say with confidence that we must not suspend the laws of sound hermeneutics when we address the topic of music. It's a problem, and I need to say so out loud.

Rather than torturing historical narratives to make points about worship music, why don't we instead use the book of the Bible that explicitly addresses worship music—the Psalms? Which brings me to a final point.

I Contradicted the Bible to Support My Music Standards

Many of the arguments I have made in the past in favor of conservative music were worse than extrabiblical; they were *unbiblical*. What I mean is, the standards I raised—against percussion, for example, or clapping, or hand-raising—could be used to criticize the Psalms. And here's a tip: If your arguments against contemporary worship could be leveled against the Psalms, you need to check yourself.

We learn to worship from Bible examples and commands, not from allegorized history. So why ignore the Psalms when debating church music? We don't know precisely what Hebrew music sounded like. But we *do* know that clapping, shouting, and loud singing were acceptable expressions of worship (Psalm 33:1, 3; 47:1). We know that people raised their voices and

114   Charles Hodge warns, "There is a strong tendency in men to treat, as matters of conscience, things which God has never enjoined." The result is that we bring ourselves into "degrading bondage" to others. Charles Hodge, *Commentary on the Epistle to the Romans* (Grand Rapids, MI: William B. Eerdmans Publishing Company, 1994), 430. Puritan Jeremiah Burroughs writes, "If men take this power upon them to compel men to do whatever they conceive to be good, and to deny or forbear whatever they conceive to be evil, they take more power upon them than ever the Apostles took." Burroughs, 85. Also see "The Fallacy of the Slippery Slope" by John Van Gelderen: revivalfocus.org/the-fallacy-of-the-slippery-slope.

their hands (Psalm 28:2). We know that the instrumentation included percussion and at times even led to worshipful dancing (Psalm 149:3; 150:4–5)—though I'm not inclined to try it myself.

When we released a new album in 2023 from Church Works Media, *Shout Out for Joy*, I received a few emails of concern from conservative friends. I'm not at all offended. I praise the Lord for those who take worship music seriously, as I urge in my book *Theology That Sticks*. To answer the questions and try to clear up any confusion, I wrote the following explanation.[115]

> Our aim has always been to produce beautiful, Bible-saturated hymns to serve Christ's church. We haven't tried to be more or less conservative. Instead, we've endeavored to be biblical. That may sound pious, but it's true. We are whole-heartedly committed to the inerrancy, authority, and sufficiency of the Bible. We believe in the Reformation doctrine of *Sola Scriptura* and in the common doctrinal affirmation that "the Bible is our only rule of faith and practice."
>
> So, what does worship look like in the Bible? In particular, what does worship look like in the book of Psalms—the inspired hymnal and handbook which tells us how our glorious God should be praised?[116] The answer is that biblical worship is full of truth about God. It is reverent. But it is also astoundingly expressive and emotive. Sometimes we weep as we worship God. But sometimes we shout, or clap, or (dare I say it) even dance. The point is, the Psalms call us to fervency, not stoicism—to lift our hands, not to fold our arms. And so, we produced an album that, while beautiful and artistic, also reflects the deep emotion and varied instrumentation of the Psalms—including brass, strings, woodwinds, and percussion in Psalm 150.

The bottom line is this: Let's allow the Bible to have its say…truly. I've had times when I'm addressing a biblical topic and in the back of my mind I think, *I wish the Bible didn't say that.* I've also had times when I did my

---

115 *Theology That Sticks: The Life-Changing Power of Exceptional Hymns* (Church Works Media, 2022). The album *Shout Out for Joy* is available on all music streaming platforms and available for download or CD purchase at ChurchWorksMedia.com. It includes fresh new arrangements of some of our most popular songs, including "His Robes for Mine," "My Jesus, Fair," "O God, My Joy," "I Run to Christ," and "Reformation Hymn," plus others that are full of gospel truth.

116 I'm using a phrase from Michael Barrett, who calls the Psalms "a handbook and a hymnbook" for the church. Barrett, 175.

best to explain away what the Bible was clearly teaching, perhaps regarding God's sovereignty or exuberant praise. I was wrong to do this. Far better to just let the Bible speak. We don't need to fear it. When the Bible calls us to joyful, celebratory worship, let's stop arguing with it and receive the Word with joy.

A Better Way: Embracing Reverent, Whole-Hearted Celebration

Perhaps the most convincing argument I've heard regarding conservative worship music is the Bible's instruction to come into God's presence with reverence. For example, Hebrews 12:28–29 commands, "Let us offer to God acceptable worship, with reverence and awe, for our God is a consuming fire."

Amen. I believe that. Our worship must never be careless or lighthearted. Reverence is a must.

Unfortunately, I've made the mistake of assuming that reverence requires conservative music, hushed tones, and the suppression of our emotions. But is that true? Think about it: When the Psalms invite us to *shout*, or *clap*, or *dance*, are they promoting worship or worship music that is irreverent? As hard as it may be, you need to say *no*.

Were we to align our worship with the Psalms, we would discover that reverence is sometimes *crazy loud* and *shockingly expressive*. I chose Psalm 47:1–2 as the subheading for this chapter on purpose:

> Clap your hands, all peoples!
> Shout to God with loud songs of joy!
> For the LORD, the Most High, is to be feared,
> A great king over all the earth.

Does the psalmist call for reverential fear? Absolutely. Does he simultaneously call for exuberant, joyful, celebratory expressions of worship that include clapping, shouting, and loud songs? Absolutely. If that bothers us, we need to alter our sensibilities. Again, let the Bible speak!

In the past, I wrongly equated celebratory music—think, *music with a beat*—with sensuality. And music can certainly be sensual. But if listening to the Gettys, Sovereign Grace, or CityAlight stirs up sensual thoughts in you, you need to do some serious soul-searching. I'm serious.

What if the sound of the music I mentioned is just *celebratory*? What if it's just biblically expressive, like the Psalms? I love how Allen P. Ross captures the power of religious music so well in his remarkable book on worship:

> The use of music in worship is a natural extension of its force in life. It elevates the singers above their mundane experiences by heightening the tone and expression of their speech and thereby increases the celebration. It also intensifies the pathos of prayers and laments, serving as a powerfully therapeutic way of dealing with the dark riddles of life.[117]

> The sum of the matter is that the overall mood of worship should be celebration in community.[118]

A Better Way: Embracing Worship Music as a Source of Unity

Call me an idealist, but I believe worship music can foster unity in Christ's church. Now I'll admit, when I first came across someone teaching that music can contribute to a church's unity, I laughed out loud. Literally. I couldn't even fathom it. But I've been persuaded.

The hallmark verse for the importance of Christian music is Colossians 3:16. And do you know what comes before it? Some of the New Testament's clearest commands regarding unity and love in the church:

> Put on then, as God's chosen ones, holy and beloved, compassionate hearts, kindness, humility, meekness, and patience, bearing with one another and, if one has a complaint against another, forgiving each other; as the Lord has forgiven you, so you also must forgive. And above all these put on love, which binds everything together in perfect harmony. And let the peace of Christ rule in your hearts, to which indeed you were called in one body. And be thankful. (Colossians 3:12–15)

What if before we sang together as a church, we expressed this kind of love to one another? What if we brought to the topic of church music virtues like compassion, kindness, humility, meekness, patience, forbearance, and forgiveness? What if we prioritized love and peace, mindful that we're part

---

117 Allen P. Ross, *Recalling the Hope of Glory: Biblical Worship from the Garden to the New Creation* (Grand Rapids: Kregel, 2006), 254.

118 Ibid., 441.

of a unified church—"one body"? Would it not change the tone of the conversation, and maybe even its content?

So, how can we use music in a way that unites the church rather than dividing it? John Frame suggests that we develop the ability to appreciate the music of other church members: "Maintaining unity among the diversity of the church's membership requires that we defer to one another in love, being willing to sing one another's music rather than insisting on the music we most enjoy."[119]

What if you determined to stretch yourself a bit regarding the songs your church sings, provided they are biblically accurate, of course. Doing so can actually be an opportunity to love others, promote unity, and grow in your own humility and selflessness.

Now, I'm not naïve enough to think this chapter will convince everybody. Maybe it won't convince *anybody*. And that's okay. If my brothers and sisters in Christ who oppose contemporary-sounding music want to keep listening to percussion-less choirs and orchestras, I get it. I love that music! I'm blessed by that music! Most of my hymns have been recorded using a simple, conservative style of music, and I'm going to keep writing deep, theological hymns that can be sung and enjoyed in a conservative style by churches that prefer that. I'm not attacking or dismissing conservative Christian music!

But let me conclude by addressing my more conservative friends. I'm not asking you to offend your conscience, though you might prayerfully consider whether or not your conscience concerning Christian music choices is truly aligned with Scripture.[120] I'm not even asking you to change your playlist. Enjoy your music for the glory of God.

But what I *am* asking is this: Stop going beyond what Scripture clearly says. Stop tying verses to your arguments and applications where they don't fit. Stop pressing your preferences onto other people's consciences. Stop justi-

---

119   John M. Frame, *Contemporary Worship Music: A Biblical Defense* (Phillipsburg, PA: P&R Publishing, 1997), 28.

120   I was helped by Andy Naselli and J. D. Crowley's book on the conscience. The fact that some things—from a singer holding a microphone to a drum set on a church platform—made me uncomfortable didn't necessarily mean they were wrong. The concept of "calibrating the conscience" to correct its misconceptions was a great relief to me, and it may be to you, as well. Andrew David Naselli and J. D. Crowley, *Conscience: What It Is, How to Train It, and Loving Those Who Differ* (Wheaton, IL: Crossway, 2016).

fying unbiblical judgmentalism. And stop separating from faithful brothers and sisters over musical preferences.

When you don't like a particular song or recording, don't use it—but don't let your preferences sever Christian relationships. And above all else, let's—all of us—stop making the topic of worship a battleground rather than holy ground.

Grace to you.

‹ PART 4 ›

CHRISTIAN UNITY IN THE 21ST CENTURY

"The church is one and is to be one because God is one. Christians have always been characterized by their unity (Acts 4:32). The unity of Christians in the church is to be a property of the church, and a sign for the world reflecting the unity of God himself. Thus, divisions and quarrels are a peculiarly serious scandal."

—Mark Dever[121]

---

121 Mark Dever, *The Church: The Gospel Made Visible* (Nashville, TN: B&H, 2012), 16.

CHAPTER 12

THE MOST ESSENTIAL UNITY: THE LOCAL CHURCH

"I entreat Euodia and I entreat Syntyche
to agree in the Lord."
—Philippians 4:2

I grew up in a pastor's home. My dad pastored three churches in Colorado during my youth. And I loved that life—most of the time. I enjoyed hearing my dad preach, and I tried reasonably hard to pay attention, even as a kid.

But there was one dark Sunday when I didn't. I wasn't quietly daydreaming, coloring in all of the O's in the bulletin, or sleeping on the pew next to my mom (all of which happened with some regularity). No, I was cutting up with my two older brothers. The three of us were born within three years of each other, and we were "all boy." My mom deserves a medal. We all goofed off, but I was the giggler, and once I started, I couldn't rein it in. You know the feeling: You're sitting in a church pew, covering your mouth, and trying to stop laughing. Your whole body is convulsing, and the whole pew is shaking. You can't breathe, and if you do finally suck in some air, the whole church will hear you. Miserable—but also funny.

Well, on the Sunday morning in question, the three of us were even more rambunctious than usual. Mom had nursery duty or some other obligation, so we were left to our own devices while Dad preached. As we frolicked in our family pew, the unthinkable happened. For the first and only time in my life, Dad stopped his sermon, apologized to the congregation, and addressed his three boisterous boys: "Jeff, Dan, and Chris, stop talking— *right now!* We will deal with this when we get home!" We got called out…by name…from the pulpit…*during the morning worship service*. No laughing followed the public rebuke, and the details of what happened at home that afternoon are probably repressed. It wasn't awesome.

I imagine that's how Euodia and Syntyche felt that Sunday morning in Philippi. They came to church, greeted friends, sang some songs, and settled in for the reading of a new letter to their church from the apostle Paul. Three chapters in and they were feeling pretty good. Then it happened: "I entreat Euodia and I entreat Syntyche to agree in the Lord" (Philippians 4:2). They were called out…by name…in the Spirit-inspired and eternal Scriptures. How utterly humiliating. It reminds me of the Southwest Airlines commercials: "Wanna get away?!" Two thousand years later, these two women are still famous, and not in a good way. I've yet to meet a family who named a daughter after either of them.

The kicker is, these two ladies weren't villains. They had "labored side by side" with Paul—and with each other—"in the gospel" (Philippians 4:3). And yet, through gossip, or rivalry, or a simple misunderstanding— *somehow*, their relationship had broken down, so much so that it was disrupting the unity and effectiveness of the entire church, warranting Paul's rebuke. Schism breaks ministry partnership, not only among spiritual toddlers but among spiritual giants. Ask Paul and Barnabas.

As a long-time pastor and as a lover of the local church, let me make six observations about local-church unity from various New Testament passages. *Local church unity is built on the gospel, preserved by humility, modeled by godly leaders, leveraged for the Great Commission, threatened by foolish controversies, and strengthened by love for Christ.* That's a mouthful! But let's give each of these ideas just a few moments of attention.

Local-Church Unity Is Built on the Gospel (Ephesians 1–3)

Most books on church unity settle into Ephesians 4:1–6, and with good reason. We'll get there in a minute. But first we need to look at what comes *before* Ephesians 4. What we have in Ephesians 1–3 is a beautiful exposition of the gospel—the spiritual "riches" that are ours in Christ (1:7, 18; 2:4, 7; 3:8, 16). We read about election, regeneration, redemption, forgiveness, adoption, and reconciliation. It's no secret that Ephesians 1–3 is mostly *indicative* verbs—statements of fact regarding what Christ has done for us. Ephesians 4–6 follows with mostly *imperative* verbs—commands regarding how we should respond to what Christ has done for us. The order is important!

As it pertains to unity, my point is that a loving, selfless, burden-bearing church isn't built on Ephesians 4:1–6. It's built on the gospel—Ephesians 1–3. The only way we can possibly behave the way chapter 4 commands us to is to be people who have been transformed by the power of the gospel. As we learn in Ephesians 2:11–22 (and as we'll study at length in chapter 14), it's the gospel that unites people from seemingly irreconcilable backgrounds and forms them into "one new man" in the local church. So, we start with the gospel!

Now, once we've started building a united church on the gospel, we move on with…*the gospel*. I'm not being pious or theoretical. Nothing could be more practical than what I'm about to share. During my twenty-five years as a pastor, I spent most of our orientation classes for new members emphasizing that what holds and keeps a church together isn't common preferences. We're not united by our music style, our children's ministries, our preferred Bible version, our politics, our educational choices, or anything else besides the gospel. I think most churches struggle with this basic point. We assume that we gather around a unifying force—a "gravity" that holds us together. "We're the conservative music church," or "We're the contemporary music church." "We're the home-schooling church." "We're the dressy church," or "We're the casual church." "We're the politically engaged church." You get the idea.

Pastors, you need to make this an oft-repeated mantra. Say it so often people get tired of hearing it. *"We don't all have to listen to the same music. We don't all have to home school, or Christian school, or public school. We don't have to agree on alcohol. We don't have to agree on politics."*

Maybe you were with me until the last one. Let me park on politics for a moment. I spent much of my life wondering how any self-respecting, God-fearing Christian could be anything but a Republican. I still believe that between the two major parties existing historically in the United States, the Democratic platform is more aggressively secular on issues like abortion and the LGBTQ+ agenda. So, I'm a political conservative.

But I have Bible-loving friends who couldn't get themselves to vote for Donald Trump. Some didn't or won't vote for him because they don't respect him as a person. Some didn't or won't vote for him because they are more conservative than he is, and some because they are less conservative than he is. Some resent his use of Scripture as a political tool. (See, for example, his endorsement of the *God Bless the USA Bible* which includes America's founding documents and Lee Greenwood's song lyrics *in the Bible* and comes off a bit like a *Babylon Bee* piece.) Some, especially people of color and some immigrants, legitimately fear for their children in a world where he is the most powerful person on the planet. As a result, these friends have either abstained, voted third party, or voted for a Democrat.

What do I do in these cases? Well, I don't believe that it's my Christian duty to *fix* these friends. And I certainly shouldn't make their party affiliation a test of fellowship.[122]

Now, you can disagree with all of those concerns about Trump. But rather than rolling your eyes and dismissing the thoughts of fellow Christians as foolish, try to understand. Empathize. And even if it still boggles your mind that someone can see things another way, I would argue that you must simply refuse to let political preferences be a factor in your relationships.

It should be possible for those who love Jesus, value the sanctity of life, and strive to live in submission to Scripture to have varying political views. After all, Jesus' twelve disciples included both a zealot who abhorred the Roman government and a tax collector employed by the Roman government (Matthew 10:1–4)—two perspectives as divergent as any you could find in first-century Palestine. You should be able to belong to the same church even if you don't belong to the same party.

And politics is just one example. But the bigger point is, people with seriously varying opinions can worship together and practice all the New Testament "one-anothers" with grace. Why? Because unity is built on the gospel—not the gospel-*plus*.

---

122   The American church is in danger of confusing Christian interests with national interests—and especially of "rendering unto Caesar the things which are God's." And we can be sinfully schismatic over our political views. My favorite resource on this topic, and a helpful remedy, is Erwin Lutzer's book *Why the Cross Can Do What Politics Can't: When They See You, Do They See Jesus?* (Eugene, OR: Harvest House Publishers, 1999).

Local-Church Unity Is Preserved by Humility
(Ephesians 4:1-6)

Okay, *now* we arrive at Ephesians 4:1-6. The first application Paul makes about a "worthy walk" for Christians isn't about evangelism, family life, or money. It's about Christian virtues that lead to unity:

> Walk in a manner worthy of the calling to which you have been called, with all humility and gentleness, with patience, bearing with one another in love, eager to maintain the unity of the Spirit in the bond of peace. (Ephesians 4:1-3)

I'm focused primarily on the first virtue listed, because *humility* is the soil in which all the others grow. You want to be part of a united church? Humble yourself. Pray that humility will be what your church is known for. Pray that it will manifest itself in *gentleness*, especially at a time when too many Christians are gruff and harsh. Pray for yourself and your church to grow in the *patience* that makes it possible to put up with each other—what Christians have historically called *forbearance*. Pray for *love*, the chief of all Christian virtues. Pray for everyone to be intentional about seeking *peace*. Think about it. If we were people who embodied these virtues, deep unity would be possible—almost easy.

I love how Ephesians 4:3 tells us to "maintain" the unity that the Spirit has already produced in His church. We don't have to manufacture unity—just protect it. Keep from messing it up! The implication is that while unity is created by God, it's also *fragile*. Christians who don't intentionally preserve and promote unity are in danger of losing it.

To emphasize the divine source of true unity, Paul gives us a series of seven statements that demonstrate that unity is essential and schism is a scandal:

> There is one body and one Spirit—just as you were called to the one hope that belongs to your call—one Lord, one faith, one baptism, one God and Father of all, who is over all and through all and in all. (Ephesians 4:4-6)

Each of those seven unifying factors relates to what the church *believes*. That's the value of a church's doctrinal statement. Like the magnets you played with as a child, a good doctrinal statement both attracts and repels people. Those who agree can unite around the truth. Those who don't agree don't have to wonder where the church stands, nor are they welcome to come in to try to change the statement of faith. This passage highlights both Christian *doctrine* and Christian *humility* as contributors to church unity—not one or the other.

Local-Church Unity Is Modeled by Godly Leaders (1 Timothy 3, Acts 6:1–7)

Unity is the responsibility of the entire assembly. But Scripture repeatedly places extra weight on the duty of the church's leaders to foster and insist on unity.

Let's start with the elders. Have you ever noticed that the qualifications for pastors would look lousy on a resume? When choosing shepherds for His church, God doesn't mention their education, their business savvy, their ability to network, their eloquence, or their intelligence. Elders don't have to be the smartest guys in the room. But they do have to be *godly*—"above reproach" (1 Timothy 3:2; Titus 1:6–7). And throughout the qualification lists, that godliness is demonstrated in virtues like gentleness, meekness, and humility (Titus 1; 1 Timothy 3:1–7; 2 Timothy 2:24–25; 1 Peter 5:1–5). Yes, the pastor must be gifted to teach, and he must lead his family well. But the rest of the qualifications focus on the kind of man he is. You can't be a self-important jerk and also be a good pastor.

Over the years I've marveled at the way Christians tolerate abusive leaders. I did an internship under an absolute bulldog of a pastor who boasted, "I'll go through blood up to my knees to show the deacons that I run the church!" When I asked if he ever considered church planting since people drove a good hour to attend his church, he bristled: "Some men can be pious and give people away if they want. But I *got* them here, and I'm going to *keep* them here!" I learned that summer a lot about what *not* to do.

Part of that kind of top-down leadership model may have been generational, and times are changing. Good! But I continue to hear shocking stories of intimidation, manipulation, and straight-out bullying by pastors. Jesus repeatedly denounced such flawed church leadership models (Mark 10:42–45). *Pagan leaders may think like that*, Jesus would say. *But you need to be like Me—a Servant Who sacrifices Himself for others. Want to be great? Serve. Want to influence others? Wash their feet.* As my friend Ken Collier puts it, "Whoever dies with the dirtiest towel wins."

Let's move on to deacons for a moment. I have a mixed history with deacons. I've served with some who were the godliest men in the church, and they were my dear friends. The faithfulness of men who work long hours, commute through traffic, and still show up for deacons meetings, prayer meetings, and workdays amazes me. Pastors, if you have faithful deacons serving alongside you, hug them often!

But I've also worked with deacons who thought it was their job to *pull* whenever they saw me *push*. The kind of deacons that had me popping Tums before our monthly meetings. One once met me for lunch, where I found out that I was the main course. "Pastor," he said, "do you know that a dozen people have left the church in the last year? How do you feel about that?" I shared with him that I *did* know and that every time a person left it was more disappointing to me than he could even imagine. Pastors take it personally when someone leaves—sometimes more personally than we should. But then I reminded him that during that same time, *eighty* people had *joined* the church. I'll never forget his response: "Well, we figure that *God* did that!"

Now, he was right in a sense. There was some decent theology in that last perspective. It *is* God Who builds His church. But it never occurred to him that maybe *God* had led people away from our church or that *I* had been a factor in people coming to the church. He just seemed set on having an adversarial relationship. Not only was he keeping score, but he was keeping it in a way that he could use every possible outcome against me. I wish I could say that I won him over in the end.

The thing is, many churches don't really understand what a deacon is supposed to do, though Scripture is clear. The deacon's role isn't to be a watchdog who keeps tabs on the pastor. It isn't to be a decision-maker. And it isn't even to lead, which is the job of the elders/pastors/overseers. The deacon's job—as indicated by the very meaning of the term *deacon*—is to *serve*. Deacons serve the Lord and His church by performing practical duties to free up the elders for spiritual duties. Better yet, they manage ministry, getting the entire assembly involved in addressing needs that arise. They allow the pastors to "devote themselves to prayer and the ministry of the Word" (Acts 6:4). And if you look at Acts 6:1–7, where the office of deacon is first introduced, the deacons met the church's practical needs in such a way that the unity that had been lost for a time was *restored!* The deacons' job is to humbly help the pastors, serve the body, solve problems, and promote unity. What church and pastor wouldn't love to have deacons like that![123]

Local-Church Unity Is Leveraged for the Great Commission (Philippians 1:27)

We started this chapter with Paul calling out Euodia and Syntyche. I want to go back there for a moment. Part of the tragedy of their fractured friendship was that they had formerly "labored side by side" with Paul "in the gospel." Their disunity didn't only hurt them. It hurt the evangelistic ministry of the church.

Similarly, Paul urges the entire Philippian church to unity in chapter 1 of Philippians, where he again has an eye on *ministry*, not just unity:

> Only let your manner of life be worthy of the gospel of Christ, so that whether I come and see you or am absent, I may hear of you that you are standing firm in one spirit, with one mind striving side by side for the faith of the gospel. (Philippians 1:27)

The goal of Christian unity—having "one spirit" and "one mind"—isn't that believers will stand face to face, admiring one another. Rather, unity enables us to stand *side by side*, working together. And that work should most often focus on gospel advance through evangelism, discipleship, and missions.

Christian unity enables Christian witness. And schism among believers destroys it. So, Paul's goal wasn't just to get Euodia and Syntyche to stop taking swings at each other. He wasn't hoping that they'd just meet up for coffee on occasion. He wanted them to get back to work, laboring "side by side...in the gospel." And if they needed "help" to get back to that point, so be it (Philippians 4:3).

Following Paul's call to unified service in Philippians 1:27, verses 28–30 go on to remind the church that we have *real enemies* outside the church. We need each other, which means we need to stop fighting each other.

---

123   If you're looking for a "starter kit" on healthy church leadership, I'd start with The Deliberate Church by Mark Dever and Paul Alexander and two books by Alexander Strauch: *Biblical Eldership* and *The New Testament Deacon*.

Time and space prohibit me from unpacking Philippians 2, but this is the "secret sauce" for church unity. How can you work "side by side" with the annoying people in your church? (And how can they tolerate *you*?) Paul tells us: We stand together for gospel advance only as we think and serve and humble ourselves like the Lord Jesus Christ (Philippians 2:1–11). We need the mind of Christ to become the mind of Christians—our way of thinking.

Local-Church Unity Is Threatened by Foolish Controversies (1–2 Timothy)

I was recently in a meeting in which a younger man listened to a new recording of a Christian song and concluded, "Certainly nobody could get offended by *that!*" The older men in the room chuckled at his naïveté and responded, "You seriously underestimate the ability of Christians to get offended." It's true. We Christians often have thin skin and quick triggers. Early in my ministry, I actually thought that being easily offended was a virtue.

Scripture teaches that silly controversies hurt the church. I'm going to cherry-pick my way through 1 and 2 Timothy, highlighting two motifs related to this issue.

First, Timothy was repeatedly commanded to pay attention to Scripture and sound doctrine (1 Timothy 1:3, 10; 4:6, 11, 13, 16; 5:17; 6:2–3; 2 Timothy 2:2, 15, 24; 4:2). He was responsible to study the Scriptures, teach them to others, and refute false teachers. Interestingly, there are no miracles in the pastoral epistles—just lots and lots of teaching.

Second, Timothy was commanded to stop fighting over dumb stuff—my description, not Paul's, though he does come close (1 Timothy 1:4, 6–7; 2:8; 4:7; 6:3–5; 2 Timothy 2:14, 23; see also Titus 1:10). I'm going to write out a few of these verses because this is so important.

> [A schismatic] is puffed up with conceit and understands nothing. He has an unhealthy craving for controversy and for quarrels about words, which produce envy, dissension, slander, evil suspicions, and constant friction among people who are depraved in mind and deprived of the truth. (1 Timothy 6:4–5)

> Remind them of these things, and charge them before God not to quarrel about words, which does no good, but only ruins the hearers. (2 Timothy 2:14)

> Have nothing to do with foolish, ignorant controversies; you know that they breed quarrels. (2 Timothy 2:23)

Paul spends a lot of ink warning Timothy—and us—about stupid things that distract and divide. Controversies. Quarrels. Myths. Dissensions. Friction. And all of it is worse than useless: it "ruins the hearers" (2 Timothy 2:14).

As a young man I had curiously strong opinions about *everything*—and I loved to debate with fellow Christians. (Cue the video of Michael Buffer shouting, *"Let's get ready to rumble!!!"*) I'd argue over a preacher I liked, a song or a book I didn't like, a conference or college I deemed too conservative or too liberal, whether churches should have choirs, whether AWANA was selling out, and whether a deacon who attended a Garth Brooks concert should be reprimanded.

In hindsight, the actual issues were only tangentially important—winning arguments was the attraction. I've noticed that older pastors often (not always) tend to soften a bit—asking fewer questions during ordination councils and engaging in fewer back-and-forth debates about ministry minutiae. The old guys have learned that quarrels and intramural skirmishes do nothing to strengthen the church or reach the lost.

Stop fighting over dumb stuff.

Local-Church Unity Is Strengthened by Love for Christ (John 21:15-17)

We'll end with Jesus' words to Peter in John 21:15–17. This passage has kept me going in ministry when everything else in my brain was telling me to quit.

There's a lot happening in John 21. The risen Christ is in pursuit of the fallen and humiliated Peter. Peter goes back to his old job. The disciples strike out during an overnight fishing trip. And Jesus reminds them of His miraculous powers through a huge haul of fish.

But the focus is on Jesus' three questions, which likely were intended to parallel Peter's three denials. Jesus asks Peter, three times, "Do you love me?" And each time that Peter says "Yes," Jesus says, "Feed my sheep."

I'm not going to get into the varying words for love or sheep. Sometimes we miss the forest for the trees—or the leaves. The big idea is this: Each time Peter says he loves Jesus, Jesus tells him to take care of Jesus' sheep. There's a life-changing lesson in that. *Your love for Jesus will keep you committed to the local church even when your love for the local church or its most difficult members is waning.*

I can be stubborn like Peter. I can fall like Peter. And after decades of pastoral ministry, I can get exasperated by Christ's church. There are times when I don't even *like* sheep. Who knew that they could kick and bite in addition to wandering off? Sometimes Christians can be downright mean!

But we don't love Christians because they're lovable, or even likable. We love them because we love Jesus. He's easy to love, even when they aren't. And He says that we show our love for Him by taking care of His flock. We love *Him* by loving *His*. As usual, Spurgeon says it better than I can: "Unless I can leave off loving Jesus Christ, I cannot cease loving those who love him…. I will defy you, if you have any love to Jesus Christ, to pick or choose among His people."[124]

Around fifteen years ago I wrote a hymn called "I Love the Church."[125] But during an especially challenging time in recent years I commented to a friend, "I couldn't write that hymn today." The church had worn me out.

And yet, the Scripture is unchanged. The primary means through which God still works in the world is the local church—not the seminary, mission board, or publishing house. "I will build My church," Jesus said. "Love me by loving My church," He said. "By this all men will know that you are My disciples—by your love for My church," He said.

After further reflection, the last line of my hymn is actually the very medicine my spirit needs: "I love the church because I love her Lord."

---

124 Lyrics from "I Love the Church" by Chris Anderson and Greg Habegger. ©2013 Church Works Worship (ASCAP) (adm at IntegratedRights.com). All rights reserved. Used by permission. Download a free hymn version: churchworksmedia.com/product/i-love-the-church-free.

125 Charles Spurgeon, sermon 668, "Unity in Christ," in The Complete Works of C. H. Spurgeon, vol. 12, (Cleveland, OH: Pilgrim, 2013).

CHAPTER 13

THE FORGOTTEN VIRTUE OF DEFERENCE

"Let not the one who eats despise the one who abstains, and let not the one who abstains pass judgment on the one who eats, for God has welcomed him."

—Romans 14:3

"In essentials, unity. In non-essentials, liberty. In all things, charity."

I've heard that statement all my life, and I love it. It's been attributed to a number of people, but as best I can tell, it originated with a guy named Rupertus Meldenius (1582–1651). It's a great saying from a guy with a great name.

Rupertus' counsel is helpful, though it's not easy to pull off. One reason is that we have a hard time distinguishing between "essentials" and "non-essentials." With that in mind, I've written a more realistic version of the saying based on my experience:

"In essentials, unity. In non-essentials, liberty. In all things, charity. EVERYTHING IS ESSENTIAL!!!"

Joking aside, the only way Christians are going to enjoy the love and unity God intends is if we learn how to differ on personal convictions and opinions without waging a war. We need to cultivate the virtue of *deference*—defined as "respectful submission or yielding to the judgment... of another."[126] Deference doesn't mean we *agree* or that our own opinions don't matter. It just means that we *disagree humbly*, without ruining a relationship.

---

126 dictionary.com/browse/deference.

I've mentioned how early fundamentalists allowed divergent opinions on important but non-essential matters. And I've used the imagery of a dimmer switch to illustrate how we can have levels of fellowship—not a binary "all or nothing." But I want to press into the concept of deference a bit more, encouraging deference in two key areas: differing *standards* and differing *doctrines*. But first, let's look at the historical source of those differences in the first-century Roman church.

The Backstory of the Disagreements in the Roman Church

The book of Romans was written to help unite a diverse church in the capital city of Rome. Christians from Jewish and Gentile backgrounds were members of the same assembly. But attending the same church and sitting in the same room doesn't mean you have the same mind. There were serious factions in the Roman church.

Unity in the midst of cultural and ethnic diversity is always a challenge, but the problem was even more pronounced in Rome. Acts 18:2 tells us that Jews were expelled from Rome by the emperor Claudius. While this description of the expulsion initially seems like only a backstory for Priscilla and Aquila, it also provides insight for the challenges faced by the Roman church. Tom Schreiner explains:

> The dismissal of the Jews from Rome in A.D. 49 had a significant effect on Roman churches. With the ejection of the Jews the churches in Rome became mainly Gentile. These Gentile house churches developed for a number of years apart from Jewish influence.[127]

In the Jews' absence, Gentile Christians were left alone in the church. And when their Jewish brothers were allowed to return some five years later, some controversy was inevitable, as Craig Blomberg relates:

> *For a full five years the church would have been almost exclusively Gentile.* Suddenly, significant numbers of Jewish believers, many of whom preceded the Gentiles in coming to faith and hoped to build up the Roman congregation, would have returned. It is only natural to imagine that many of these people might have wanted their leadership roles back. Even if not, the assimilation of a sudden influx of

---

127   Thomas R. Schreiner, *Romans, Baker Exegetical Commentary on the New Testament* (Grand Rapids, MI: Baker Books, 1998), 13.

new people from a rival ethnic group is never an easy task for any church. No doubt some of the tensions between Jewish and Gentile Christians were not entirely resolved three years later in 57, and *a large part of Paul's purpose in writing would be to try to unify these different factions.*[128]

So, Paul writes in order to help bridge the chasm between the two groups. Of course, the book of Romans is the classic delineation of justification by faith. But it also has much to say about peaceful relationships in Christ's church. Schism is such a scandal to our Lord that He inspired the greatest tome on the meaning and power of the gospel in order to promote unity within His church!

That's why Paul spends Romans 1–3 pointing out that all people are sinners: Gentile pagans (chapter 1), Jewish hypocrites (chapter 2), everybody, including us (chapter 3). "All y'all," as we say in Atlanta.

Once again, it's the gospel that brings lasting unity. So, Paul spends chapters 4–8 of Romans describing justification by faith, union with Christ, the struggle with our flesh, the life-changing power of the Spirit, and the unbreakable love of God. He then spends chapters 9–11 describing God's gracious plan to graft Gentiles into the Jewish tree. As difficult as those chapters are, they reveal the unfathomable grace and wisdom of God. And both sections are *full* of implications for unity in the Roman church.

Romans 12 is the "hinge" that turns the book from practical *doctrine* to doctrinal *practice*. Once again, indicative verbs give way to imperative verbs. That is, what Christ has done for us leads to our responsibilities to Him and one another. Chapter 12 is a beautiful description of "life in the body," the local church. Paul tells the Roman believers to use their spiritual gifts to build up the body, much as he does in 1 Corinthians 12. But he especially urges them to care for one another:

> Let love be genuine. Abhor what is evil; hold fast to what is good. Love one another with brotherly affection. Outdo one another in showing honor. Do not be slothful in zeal, be fervent in spirit, serve the Lord. Rejoice in hope, be patient in tribulation, be constant in prayer. Contribute to the needs of the saints and seek to show hospitality. Bless

---

128 Craig L. Blomberg, *From Pentecost to Patmos* (Nashville, TN: B&H Academic, 2006), 235. Emphases in original.

those who persecute you; bless and do not curse them. Rejoice with those who rejoice, weep with those who weep. Live in harmony with one another. Do not be haughty, but associate with the lowly. Never be wise in your own sight. Repay no one evil for evil, but give thought to do what is honorable in the sight of all. If possible, so far as it depends on you, live peaceably with all. (Romans 12:9–18)

Knowing the ethnic and cultural fissures in the Roman church (and in our own!), I think we can understand God's wisdom in those Romans 12 instructions: *Jews and Gentiles—love one another. Compete to be the one who shows the most honor to those across the aisle. Wealthy people, assist the poor...regardless of their ethnicity. Jews, be hospitable to Gentiles, and vice versa. Show hospitality to each other. When someone has a cause for joy, celebrate with them. And when someone has a broken heart, weep with them. Put away the foolish pride that keeps you at arm's length from the lowly. And if there's a schism, don't let it be your fault. Seek peace.*

He returns to the topic of mutual love among believers in the latter half of chapter 13. If it seems like he's cycling, it's because these exhortations were desperately needed, both in their day and in ours.

Owe no one anything, except to love each other, for the one who loves another has fulfilled the law. For the commandments, "You shall not commit adultery, You shall not murder, You shall not steal, You shall not covet," and any other commandment, are summed up in this word: "You shall love your neighbor as yourself." Love does no wrong to a neighbor; therefore love is the fulfilling of the law. (Romans 13:8–10)

Deference When We Have Differing Standards

After an important series of commands related to fighting their own sin, from lust and drunkenness to quarreling and jealousy, Paul arrives at Romans 14:1–15:7, Scripture's premier passage on Christian deference.

Give the passage a slow read. Especially pay attention to how the issues in question primarily deal with the divergent lifestyles and customs of Jewish and Gentile Christians—debatable issues like the eating of meat and the observance of special days.

Romans 14 urges unity amid diverse opinions. The overarching theme of the passage isn't meat or days, but Christian unity. Better, Paul is arguing for Christian *fellowship*—not just tolerance, but deep affection. And so he begins and ends the passage with the same "bookend" command: "Welcome each other" (14:1; 15:7). The idea is acceptance, approval, intimacy—open arms that reveal open hearts. The opposite of welcoming a brother or sister with different habits or standards than your own can be seen in the negative words Paul uses throughout the passage: *quarreling, judging, despising, tripping,* and *destroying.*

Romans 14 addresses issues of conscience—not biblical prohibitions. We can be certain that when Paul exhorts the Romans to welcome one another in spite of disagreements, he is addressing only issues of conscience, not issues where the Bible has made explicit prohibitions. Paul doesn't tell them to tolerate each other's immorality, for example. He expressly forbids immorality (13:13–14).

But the issues in Romans 14 are different. He is discussing practices that are *amoral,* not *immoral*: whether someone eats meat (14:2, 6, 15, 17, 20, 21), whether someone observes certain days as holy (14:5, 6), or whether someone drinks wine (14:17, 21). Paul's instruction is for each believer to make up his own mind on these controversial topics (14:2, 5) and to guard his own conscience (14:22–23). And the assumption is that people will land in different places, which this passage says is fine!

Think about it. Paul had the perfect opportunity to tell every Christian to adopt the most conservative position possible, just to be safe. But he didn't. He avoided teaching what I call an "ethic of avoidance"—an austere asceticism. He avoided legalistic rules. He didn't make everything black and white, but opted instead for discernment, liberty, and charity. And he did all of this under the inspiration of the Spirit!

Romans 14 argues that God is fine with believers on both sides of these issues. Notice Paul's insistence that *God* has "welcomed" members on both sides of the issues (14:3; 15:7). Remember—these observations bookend the passage, and they give further proof that the practices in question are not forbidden by Scripture. But the force of Paul's argument couldn't be stronger: *If God has received your brother in fellowship despite a practice that annoys you, how can you not likewise receive that brother? Are your standards higher than God's?*

Throughout the passage, Paul keeps reiterating that the judge of other Christians' behavior is *God—not you!* Again, the argument is exceptionally strong. *Who do you think you are? Do you think God needs your help? Worry about yourself. God is the Judge of us all.* Let me cite a few examples of this reasoning, with added emphasis:

> Why do you pass judgment on your brother? Or you, why do you despise your brother? For we will all stand before the judgment seat of *God.*
>
> Each of us will give an account of himself *to God.*
>
> Who are you to pass judgment on the servant of another? It is before his own *master* that he stands or falls. And he will be upheld, for the *Lord* is able to make him stand. (Romans 14:10, 12, 14)

The gist of Paul's instruction is to "stay in your lane." One of the Baptist distinctives (also held by many non-Baptist churches) is the autonomy of the local church and the responsibility of each local church's God-ordained elders to shepherd the particular flock over which the Holy Spirit has made them overseers (Acts 20:28)—*not other flocks.* Add to this the distinctive of "individual soul liberty," and we have sufficient motivation to stop insisting that other churches and other Christians live according to the dictates of *our* consciences, especially on issues where the Bible allows diverse opinions. In the words of 1 Thessalonians 4:11, "Mind your own business" (Chris Anderson Version. All rights reserved.).

If God approves of our brothers and sisters, how dare we disapprove? If God receives our brothers and sisters despite their diversity of backgrounds, opinions, and habits, so must we.

Romans 14 argues for mutual charity, not selfishness. Having urged Christians to respect each other's freedom of choice on amoral issues, Paul also encourages believers to be selfless, even in the exercise of their liberties. Don't cause a brother to stumble (14:13–16, 21). Don't wreck the work of God just so you can do what you please (14:17–20). This should go without saying, but *love others more than you love your liberties.*

Now, Paul's not saying that nobody should eat meat, drink wine, or observe days in order to avoid offending anyone. That would undo the entire passage. Nor is he arguing that everyone must eat meat, drink wine, or observe days. Instead, he leaves the uncomfortable differences of opinion alone and argues for *deference*. But, there are occasions, he says, when you should curb your liberties to avoid tripping up a brother or sister.

Put it this way: If I'm a pork-eating Gentile, I can enjoy my bacon. But if a weak-conscienced Jewish brother is coming over for dinner, I shouldn't serve a BLT—at least not at that particular meal. More applicably for most of us, if I have the liberty in my conscience to have a glass of wine with my meal, I can do so with thanksgiving, even if other brothers and sisters can't in their own consciences. But if a recovering alcoholic comes for dinner, I should serve Coke, at least at that meal.

Romans 14 shows how differences can actually lead us to glorify God. Finally, at stake in this discussion is not only the private practices of Christians, but the glory of God. Those who enjoy meat and those who don't enjoy meat should do so with thanksgiving (14:6ff; compare 1 Corinthians 10:31). The overall goal of extending deference to one another isn't just an uncomfortable peace—it's that *together* we might give glory to God (15:5–6). Again, Paul's aim is extremely high. Don't just put up with each other. Join your hearts and voices in giving praise to God!

> May the God of endurance and encouragement grant you to live in such harmony with one another, in accord with Christ Jesus, that together you may with one voice glorify the God and Father of our Lord Jesus Christ. (15:5–6)

I love this word from John Owen: "When men have laboured as much in the improvement of the principle of forbearance as they have done to subdue other men to their opinions, religion will have another appearance in the world."[129] The unity of Christians who, outside of Christ, would be rivals is the church's ultimate apologetic to a watching world.

Deference When We Have Differing Doctrines

We've discussed the concept of doctrinal triage throughout the book. I've noted that the genius of early fundamentalism was its ability to differentiate

---

129   John Owen, *The Works of John Owen*, ed. William H. Gould (Carlisle, PA: The Banner of Truth Trust, 1967), 13:95.

between essential doctrines that required lockstep agreement and second- or third-tier matters on which they could agree to disagree. Even long-time Bob Jones University president and chancellor, Bob Jones, Jr., recognized this point:

> [The Bob Jones University] Creed sets forth the great fundamentals of the faith held by all Bible believers. Godly Christians may differ on what the Scripture teaches about some things and may not agree on the interpretation of certain doctrines; but upon the great fundamental truths set forth in the "Bob Jones University Creed," they are in complete agreement. These are the essential doctrines, the foundation of Christian faith.[130]

Whether Bob Jones, Jr. or the university have always operated by that "godly-Christians-may-differ" statement, the ideal was at least acknowledged. Fifty years later, and in a different corner of the vineyard, Collin Hansen writes something very similar: "At its best, evangelicalism overcomes nonessential differences to unite like-minded Christians around the common cause of gospel proclamation and gospel living."[131]

Gavin Ortlund's book *Finding the Right Hills to Die on: The Case for Theological Triage* is a helpful guide on the matter of doctrinal differences. I don't always agree with his topography—which "hills" are worth fighting for—but he writes with both clarity and charity. He has a category for essential doctrines on which variance in opinion is intolerable. But he also believes we're too quick to cut ties over less important matters of interpretation, and I tend to agree. He writes,

> Most of the battles you *could* fight, you shouldn't. And I'd go so far as to say that the majority of doctrinal fights Christians have today tend to be over third-rank issues—or fourth. We deeply need to cultivate greater doctrinal forbearance, composure, and resilience.[132]

The concept of theological deference has been illustrated using a variety of images. Ortlund uses "hills." I've suggested a dimmer switch. Francis

---

130 Bob Jones, Jr., *Fundamentals of Faith* (Greenville, SC: Bob Jones University Press, 1962) 1.

131 Collin Hansen, "Introduction" in *Four Views on the Spectrum of Evangelicalism*, ed. Andrew David Naselli and Collin Hansen (Grand Rapids, MI: Zondervan, 2011), 10.

132 Ortlund, 125. Another resource which has shaped my thinking on the virtue of deference is Andy Naselli and J. D. Crowley's book *The Conscience: What It Is, How to Train It, and Loving Those Who Differ* (Wheaton, IL: Crossway, 2016).

Schaeffer uses a hierarchy.[133] Al Mohler uses medical triage.[134] Justin Taylor uses a target.[135] Dick and Rick Gregory use a pyramid.[136] My pastor, Brian Peterson, uses "top shelf" for essential doctrines, "second shelf" for denominational distinctives, and "bottom shelf" for matters of personal persuasion and conscience. All these images are helpful, and they all have in common the idea that levels of agreement affect levels of cooperation.

Core doctrines—what have been called *the fundamentals*—must be believed to be a Christian. If one rejects the inspiration of Scripture, the virgin birth, the deity of Christ, the vicarious atonement, the resurrection, justification by faith alone, or the Trinity, he or she is unchristian and we can have no spiritual connection. Mohler writes, "These first-order doctrines represent the most fundamental truths of the Christian faith, and a denial of these doctrines represents nothing less than an eventual denial of Christianity itself."[137]

Important doctrines must be agreed upon for deeper partnerships. One can be a Christian and vary on these issues, but they're important enough that disagreement on any one of them might preclude serving together in the same church. Examples of mid-level doctrines include baptism, church polity, cessationism vs. continuationism, complementarianism vs. egalitarianism, and dispensationalism vs. covenant theology. Based on my particular ministry milieu, I've included some issues here that others assign to the next category.

Peripheral issues are matters where there may be variance within a church, a leadership team, or even a marriage. Members of the church at Rome disagreed on issues like these and were commanded to enjoy fellowship anyway. These issues aren't *un*important—just not *as* important as the issues listed above. I'd assign to this section issues like how "Calvinistic"

---

133   Schaeffer, 90–91.

134   Albert Mohler, "A Call for Theological Triage and Christian Maturity," July 12, 2005, albertmohler.com/2005/07/12/a-call-for-theological-triage-and-christian-maturity/. Also see Mohler's chapter "Confessional Evangelicalism" in *Four Views on the Spectrum of Evangelicalism*.

135   Justin Taylor, "Levels of Doctrine," The Gospel Coalition, March 17, 2010, thegospelcoalition.org/blogs/justin-taylor/how-do-you-evaluate-and-weigh-the-importance-of-various-doctrines/.

136   Gregory and Gregory, 16.

137   Mohler, "A Call for Theological Triage."

one is, one's preferred Bible version, one's preferred music style, and even the minute details of one's eschatology. Lifestyle choices like holiday celebrations, tattoos, and alcohol can fit in this category as well.

I'm not suggesting that my model is perfect. The category to which an issue gets assigned will differ depending on a person's ministry setting and the weight that person places on that particular issue. The vast majority of us would agree that the first-tier issues are basically set: the fundamentals. But many might disagree about lines drawn between second- and third-level issues. In any case, it's helpful to have a grid to help you think through which issues should be deal-breakers for you—"the right hills to die on."

To responsibly promote church unity while simultaneously preserving church purity, we *must* learn to distinguish between essential and nonessential issues. When fundamental doctrines are at stake, it's time to *defend*. But when personal preferences are in play, it's time to *defer*. Good people differ, and we should extend grace to one another.

Al Mohler writes,

> We must develop the skill of discerning different levels of theological issues in order that we not divide over the wrong issues and betray the gospel. But when the issues are of the first order, we must be clear and determined, lest we lose the gospel.[138]

By God's grace, I'm working on the forgotten virtue of deference. I haven't arrived, to be sure. Candidly, I've become more comfortable over the years deferring to Christians on my left—people who may be less conservative than me on some issues but who share a love for Christ, for expository preaching, for reformed soteriology, and so on. Conversely, I've tended to roll my eyes at Christians on my right—people who still use the King James Version, who have more traditional services, or who minimize election.

But the Lord has convicted me about these attitudes, revealing to me my own schismatic spirit. If we truly believe that the gospel is both the source of Christian unity and the rally point for Christian cooperation, we should be able to fellowship and partner with orthodox believers on both our right and our left. We should be able to extend deference both ways, as long as

---

138 Mohler, "Confessional Evangelicalism," 96.

doing so doesn't erode essential Christian doctrines. Put it this way: *I can eat with you. Can you eat with me?*

Charles Hodge writes with deep conviction on the deference called for in Romans 14. He urges Christians to show each other charity and to avoid being a stumbling block. But he also warns against yielding your conscience to anyone "but to truth and God."[139] Indeed, he argues that sometimes the only right response to unnecessary, extrabiblical standards is to *contradict* them, as Christ did with the Pharisees' hedging around the Sabbath. But it is Hodge's conclusion regarding Christian unity that I find to be especially profound:

> The fellowship of the saints is not to be broken for unessential matters.... Christians should not allow anything to alienate them from their brethren, who afford credible evidence that they are the servants of God. Owing to ignorance, early prejudice, weakness of faith, and other causes, there may and must exist a diversity of opinion and practices on minor points of duty. But this diversity is no sufficient reason for rejecting from Christian fellowship any member of the family of Christ.[140]

I long to be able to quote Psalm 119:63 with a clear conscience: "I am a companion of *all* who fear you, of those who keep your precepts." Don't you?

---

139 Hodge, 430.

140 Ibid., 428–29.

CHAPTER 14

RACIAL SCHISM AND AMERICA'S MOST SEGREGATED HOUR

*"For he himself is our peace, who has made us both one
and has broken down in his flesh
the dividing wall of hostility."*

—Ephesians 2:14

There was a time when I believed that the world was doing better with racial issues than the church was. Schools, workplaces, and sporting events boasted diversity. Most churches didn't. In the words of Martin Luther King, Jr., Sunday morning continued to be "the most segregated hour" of American life.[141]

The last few years have changed my opinion. It's not that the church is doing much better. It's just that the world's celebration of ethnic diversity was revealed to be a façade. After the death of George Floyd in 2020 (and too many others), the riots that followed, and the partisan responses to such tragedies, it's clear that the world merely papered over the problem of systemic racism. America is dealing with racial tensions that may lack the day-to-day violence of the 1960s but are nevertheless very real.

America's racial divide is a problem for the *church* as well. Perhaps no contemporary issue is the cause of deeper schism in the church than the inability of differing ethnicities and cultures to coexist and even thrive within the same local assembly. Our division along ethnic lines is particu-

---

141   Martin Luther King, Jr. on Meet the Press, April 17, 1960. youtube.com/watch?v=1q881g1L_d8&t=33s.

larly tragic because *the church has the answer*. We can actually fix this, at least within our sphere of influence. I love the statement made by a multiethnic church in Denver: "Racism is an illness. Only Jesus is the cure."[142] Hear John Piper's burden about the world's impotence and the gospel's power:

> Religious tradition and human opinion are powerless to create and sustain a life of Christ-exalting ethnic diversity and harmony. Only a deeply rooted grasp of what God has achieved through the gospel of Jesus can do this.[143]

It's time for Christians to stop justifying ourselves by saying, "We're no worse than the world." Instead, we should confess, "We're no better than the world"—or not much better. Christian musician Shai Linne writes, "Has it not often been the case, both historically and presently, that the fault lines of ethnic division in the church and the world are indistinguishable?"[144] It's time for the church to raise the bar and to show the world the way forward. That's not to say it will be easy. I'm no blind optimist. I pastored a church in the deep South, and I can attest that the struggle of racism is real.

I've had a deacon and school board member ask me if it bothered me that "a black boy" hugged one of my daughters at a soccer game.

I've had a church leader respond to my inviting a black waiter to join us at church by saying to me in hushed tones, "Those people don't want to worship with us."

I've heard of a pastor who said, from the pulpit, "I'm not defending the KKK, but...." (There's no decent way to finish that sentence.)

I've felt the pressure on an African American lady and her daughter who joined our church but were sometimes called "sellouts" for attending a "white church."

---

142 Manuel Ortiz, *One New People: Models for Developing a Multiethnic Church* (Downers Grove, IL: IVP Academic), 57.

143 John Piper, *Bloodlines* (Wheaton, IL: Crossway, 2011), 211.

144 Shai Linne, *The New Reformation: Finding Hope in the Fight for Ethnic Unity* (Chicago, IL: Moody Publishers, 2021), 15.

I've had a successful black church member tell me that when he runs in his nice suburban neighborhood, he always wears shorts and never wears a hoodie, lest he be suspected of robbery.

I've hurt for my white daughter and black son-in-law when they've received dirty looks—from both white and black people—or when my son-in-law was called "white boy" for being in public with my family.

I've had church members complain that I was "politically correct" or "woke" because I spoke out in opposition to the senseless killing of George Floyd—though I also spoke out in opposition to the senseless riots that followed it. I sympathize with Lig Duncan who said during an Atlanta conference, "If you're against racism, somebody will accuse you of being woke."

All is not well. I get it.

Voddie Baucham, in his controversial but insightful book *Fault Lines*, writes the following:

> The current cultural moment is precarious. The United States is on the verge of a race war, if not a complete cultural meltdown. And the rest of the Western world seems to be following suit. Tensions are rising in every place the African slave trade has left its indelible mark.[145]

And yet, we have every reason for optimism. The church I pastored in Atlanta has an exceptionally diverse school—40% black, 30% white, and 30% Spanish, Asian, and Indian—and the students get along beautifully. The church is beginning to reflect its community as well. During my final year there, new members included a black family, an Indian family, a Romanian man married to a Mexican woman, a Hispanic young man married to an Asian young lady, a white man married to a Filipino lady, and so on. The church's newest pastoral hires are a Hispanic man and an African American man—so there's diversity in leadership, not just membership. My optimistic vision is being played out, by God's grace: *If we reach our community, we will reflect our community.*

---

145 Voddie T. Baucham, Jr. *Fault Lines: The Social Justice Movement and Evangelicalism's Looming Catastrophe* (Washington, D.C.: Salem Books, 2021), 5. The primary goal of Baucham's book is to warn evangelicals of the "cult" of Critical Race Theory. He exposes the unbiblical tenets of CRT and argues, among other things, that statistics regarding police brutality against black men are intentionally inflated by social justice warriors. There is clearly a racial problem in America, but while Baucham acknowledges the need, he urges more integrity and intentionally biblical thinking in the pursuit of true justice. It's a helpful, if unsettling, read.

After finishing my pastorate at that church, I attended a church plant in inner-city Atlanta. It's *crazy* diverse. On staff were two preaching pastors—one white and one black—as well as a Spanish pastor, my black son-in-law, and others. Our community group had one white family—*mine*—and I've honestly never had such rich, Bible-centered fellowship with a small group. Oh, and the church navigated through the merger of a young and diverse body with an aging white congregation in the area. Successfully! By God's grace, I think this is happening more and more often.

But I'm not only optimistic because of progress made in two Southern churches. I'm optimistic because the Bible has the answer to the problem of racism. The ethnic tensions in America and around the world provide for us a great opportunity to show the deep and pervasive unity that the gospel alone can bring. As my friend J. D. Crowley puts it, "The gospel of Jesus Christ will plunge a cross-shaped dagger right into the heart of racism."[146]

Let's take a look at some Bible passages that show us a way forward.

All Humanity Is United by Creation (Genesis 1; Acts 17:26; 1 Corinthians 15:22–23)

The first way to battle racism is to stop thinking of people as inherently different. Genesis teaches that all humanity was made in the image of God (Genesis 1:26–27; 9:6). In Acts 17:26, Paul (a Jew) preaches to the Areopagus Court in Athens (Gentiles) that "every nation of mankind" was made by God "from one man." Despite some relatively minor physical eccentricities, we're all the same. We're all family, descending from our great-great-grandparents, Adam and Eve. In fact, Paul argues in 1 Corinthians 15:22 that all of humanity's union in Adam and all of the elect's union in Christ are essential to our salvation: "For as in Adam all die, so also in Christ shall all be made alive." (See Romans 5:12–21.)

Humanity is all the same. That's why I don't even like using the term "race" in these discussions. There's only one human race. Occasionally, I'll get asked if I'm opposed to interracial marriage. It's an unfortunate question, really. Why is it even in doubt? Anyway, I nearly always have a little fun with my answer. *Interracial marriage? You mean a man who marries his cat? Gross! Oh, but if you mean a black man and a white lady or vice versa, I'm*

---

146   J. D. Crowley, "Check It Off the List" in *Gospel Meditations for Missions* (Church Works Media, 2011), Day 6.

completely in favor. You realize that there's only one human race, right? I'm only opposed to interfaith marriage (1 Corinthians 7:39; 9:5).

Despite a culture that keeps exaggerating our differences and capitalizing on class and ethnic divides, we're the same. We share God's image. We share grandparents, and we share their guilt. We share our human nature, as Carl Trueman ably writes:

> All humans are partakers of a common human nature. All are addressed by the same revelation of the same God, and all are called to respond to that revelation.... Human nature is not simply a sociolinguistic construct. It has an ineradicable [irremovable] reality; and that reality provides the vital point of contact across cultures, times, ethnicities, genders, sexual orientations, skin colors, and whatever other particulars we might care to think up. Indeed, to deny this would be to subvert the theology that Paul expresses in his Adam-Christ parallelism and would thus dramatically impact the nature of salvation. In fact, it would abolish Pauline soteriology in its entirety.[147]

All Humanity Is United in the Local Church (Acts 11, 13)

Someday I'm going to write a book on the church at Antioch. Someday. But for now, I'll write just a few paragraphs that are pertinent to this racial schism discussion. Antioch is my favorite church in the New Testament. It was a gospel powerhouse. And it was an ethnic melting pot from its inception (Acts 11:19–26).

I love Alexander Maclaren's summary of the anonymous brothers' executive decision to evangelize everybody, not just Jews:

> As they saw [Antioch's] swarming multitudes, [they] felt that the restriction of the message to Jews was clean contrary to the spirit of the Gospel, and so defied precedent, and out of the mere promptings of the Christian spirit, took the leap which Peter needed a special command to dare.... They probably did not at all realize what a great

---

147   Carl Trueman, *Crisis of Confidence: Reclaiming the Historic Faith in a Culture Consumed with Individualism and Identity* (Wheaton, IL: Crossway, 2024), 49–50.

step they were taking. They had the Gospel; Antioch needed it. They could not be silent.[148]

Do you remember how I said that a church that *reaches* its community will *reflect* its community? That's exactly what happened in Antioch. The city was a commercial hub on the edge of the Mediterranean. The whole world lived there. And as more and more people came to Christ, the church became as diverse as its city.

With that in mind, it shouldn't be a surprise to read of a diverse pastoral team in Acts 13:1—a guy from Cyprus (Barnabas), a guy from the Middle East (Saul), two guys from Africa (Simeon and Lucius), and a guy from the royal household in Judea (Manaen). So, two of the leaders were black: "Simeon who was called Niger" and "Lucius of Cyrene." A third was from the upper crust—Manaen was a member of the household of Herod.

There's a lot to learn here. But first, let me embarrass myself. I feel like my spiritual gift is saying stupid things, especially about diversity. When preaching on Acts 13:1 in my home church in Atlanta, I carefully explained that Simeon and Lucius were "African Americans." Brilliant, right? Never mind the fact that they never set foot in the Western hemisphere or that America was a good 1,700 years from being founded! I've also preached, with great passion, that God doesn't play favorites based on how much *melatonin* is in your skin. (Yawn.) Pray for me.

Back to Acts 13:1! It's encouraging to me that the strongest, most missions-minded church in the New Testament was a spiritual tapestry. It was as diverse as the city around it. And the diversity was reflected in its godly *leaders*, not just in its membership. It can happen, but not through lame attempts at political correctness or virtue signaling. Only the gospel can bring the kind of ethnic harmony we see in the church at Antioch, as William Hendriksen wisely points out:

> The reason why there is so much strife in this world, between individuals, families, social or political groups, whether small or large, is that the contending parties, through the fault of either or both, have not found each other at Calvary. Only when sinners have been reconciled

---

148   Alexander Maclaren, *The Acts of the Apostles* (Grand Rapids, MI: Zondervan Publishing House, 1959), 139–40.

to God through the cross will they be truly reconciled to each other.... For a world torn by unrest and friction, the gospel is the only answer.[149]

Which brings us to my favorite "diversity" passage.

All Humanity Is United by Christ's Work (Ephesians 2)

Ephesians 2 is a remarkable chapter. It begins with our spiritual deadness in verse 1, pivots on the "but God" of verse 4, then builds to salvation by grace in verses 8 and 9. Beautiful. But for most of my life, I stopped reading in verse 10. As a result, I missed the climax.

In Ephesians 2:11–22 Paul celebrates the miraculous unity that God has produced through the gospel. Specifically, he rejoices that God has bridged the chasm that separated Jews and Gentiles. Having reviewed the Gentiles' exclusion from God's people in the Old Testament (vv. 11–12), Paul pivots with a "but," just as he did in 2:4:

> But now in Christ Jesus you who once were far off have been brought near by the blood of Christ. For he himself is our peace, who has made us both one and has broken down in his flesh the dividing wall of hostility by abolishing the law of commandments expressed in ordinances, that he might create in himself one new man in place of the two, so making peace, and might reconcile us both to God in one body through the cross, thereby killing the hostility. (vv. 13–16)

There's so much gold here, and I can't begin to do it justice. But the key idea is that God hasn't only reconciled Gentiles to Himself—which is amazing—but that God has reconciled Gentiles and Jews. There is a horizontal reconciliation as well as a vertical reconciliation. That's what Paul means when he says God has "broken down...the dividing wall of hostility."

Remember, Gentiles were excluded from the Old Testament Temple. They could go to the Temple Mount, but they were kept at arm's length in the Court of the Gentiles. Lest there be any confusion, there was a stone sign posted in Jesus' time that read, "Foreigners must not enter inside the balustrade or into the forecourt around the sanctuary. Whoever is caught will have himself to blame for his ensuing death." Welcome to our church!

---

149   William Hendriksen, *New Testament Commentary: Exposition of Ephesians* (Grand Rapids, MI: Baker Academic, 2007), 136.

Think of it this way. When Jesus died, the veil in the Temple was torn from top to bottom (Matthew 27:51), signifying that the exile of sinners from God's presence that dated back to Genesis 3 had been lifted. Sinners can now approach God through Christ (Hebrews 10:19–22). But just as the veil signified access to God, the figurative tearing down of the "wall" dividing Jews and Gentiles signified the joining of Christians from all ethnicities into one church. God's grand design for the church is to make "one new [congregation of worshipers] in place of the two"—and to accomplish that peace through the blood of Christ. Unity is that important!

That's why it saddens me to see white churches, black churches, Chinese churches, and so on. That wasn't God's intent. As Mark DeYmaz describes it, we have a "biblical mandate for the multi-ethnic church"—at least in multi-ethnic communities.[150] Conrad Mbewe, dubbed "the African Spurgeon," nails it:

> We should fight against the practice of white people worshiping alone and black people worshiping alone simply because of skin color. Even when those divisions persist in our society, they should not prevail in our churches. The gospel should unite us in practice as well as principle. Our fellowship should remove all these social boundaries, because we are one in Christ. The world should see that we are different and that the gospel has broken down all these walls of hostility that find expression in our society. This is the unity that we should seek to realize.[151]

All Humanity Is United as Equals in Christ (Galatians 3:27–28)

This beautiful passage expresses the same principle we considered from Ephesians 2. But the historical setting is different. In Ephesians, Paul writes to show the power of the gospel (chs. 1–3) and to urge the church to walk in a manner consistent with the gospel (chs. 4–6). But Galatians was written in the midst of controversy. Paul again urges unity, but he does so to defend the gospel against legalists who were trying to force the Gentiles

---

150   Mark DeYmaz, *Building a Healthy Multi-Ethnic Church: Mandate, Commitments, and Practices of a Diverse Congregation* (Hoboken, NJ: Jossey-Bass, 2007), xx.

151   Mbewe, 57.

to live like Jews. And so, he says in this passage that the gospel makes human distinctions obsolete:

> For as many of you as were baptized into Christ have put on Christ. There is neither Jew nor Greek, there is neither slave nor free, there is no male and female, for you are all one in Christ Jesus. (Galatians 3:27–28)

Contrary to how it may look, Paul isn't erasing gender, ethnic, or class distinctions. A woman who trusts Christ remains a woman. A black man will always be black. And slaves in Paul's day still had to do what they were told, though he commanded that they be treated well. The point of the passage is simply that *issues like gender, ethnicity, and social standing aren't factors when it comes to the gospel.* We all trust Christ the same way. We all have the same need and the same standing. The gospel doesn't show favoritism. In Christ, regardless of other factors, we are "all one."

Years ago, Thabiti Anyabwile preached an unforgettable message on this topic at the 2008 Together for the Gospel conference. The message was titled, "Bearing the Image: Identity, the Work of Christ, and the Church."[152] The most memorable portion for me was the idea that if I enter a room full of other middle-aged white men who don't know Jesus, *we're different.* And if I enter a room full of people from a wide array of ethnicities, cultures, ages, and genders—but who all know Christ—*we're the same.* Our main identity is that we're *Christians*—not Americans, Republicans, or Caucasians. The message left a mark, and it ultimately changed the course of my family.

Let me take a moment to acknowledge that *this is hard.* I shared that the church I pastored in Atlanta was growing in its diversity. I praise the Lord for that. But for years, the black people who joined our church tended to come from Jamaica, or Haiti, or Ghana. African Americans who grew up in the South found it much harder to bridge the divide between themselves and a predominantly white church. Our nation has so much racial baggage—and it's not all from the 1800s or the 1960s. It's hard to get past prejudice *now.*

---

152 Thabiti Anyabwile, "Bearing the Image: Identity, the Work of Christ, and the Church." t4g.org/resources/thabiti-anyabwile/bearing-the-image-identity-the-work-of-christ-and-the-church-session-ii.

And as exciting as it is to see a church reflect the community on Sunday, that's still just a baby step. It's one thing to share a pew with someone who looks different from you. It's another thing to share a prayer request, to share a burden, or to share a meal in your home. When Christians of various cultures are getting together *both inside and outside of official church meetings*—that's when we'll be making real progress.

But when it happens, my, is it beautiful! And I've seen it happen in the most unlikely of places. In 2023, I was privileged to preach a series of meetings at Antioch Bible Church (love the name!) in Johannesburg, South Africa. You want to talk about a culture with racial baggage! It would be hard to find a place with more racial tension than South Africa. And yet, Antioch Bible Church is remarkably diverse. People of varying ethnicities, education levels, and cultures—people who have emerged from the travesty of Apartheid!—are united. They love each other, serve each other, laugh together, fellowship together. In the words of Galatians 3:28, they "are all one."

American's history of racism doesn't make unity in a multiethnic church impossible, just difficult. Isaac Adams, in his exceptional book *Talking About Race*, acknowledges how awkward and exhausting it can be for Christians to engage each other on these issues. But he's also biblically optimistic about what would happen if Christians of all ethnicities loved each other the way Jesus commanded and the effect such a miracle would have on a watching world:

> If we could do this, one of the hardest challenges for churches in America—loving across racial lines—could become one of their most powerful testimonies to a divided and dividing world. If we could think about our communication challenges regarding race, by God's grace, we could show the world a different world.[153]

My Baby Girl, Her Husband, and Great Grace

I want to finish this chapter by sharing my daughter's story. I have four daughters, and each of them is uniquely smart, beautiful, funny, and godly. They're best friends, which makes their parents both proud and grateful. The eldest is Rebekah. In 2019, she married Ray, one of my favorite people

---

153   Isaac Adams, *Talking About Race: Gospel Hope for Hard Conversations* (Grand Rapids, MI: Zondervan Reflective, 2022), xiii.

in the world—a great husband, son, and dad who is also an African American.

Rather than telling you their story, I'll let her do it. She wrote for her school paper when she was in college, and she used the platform to spread some knowledge.[154] Since the piece was published—and shared all over social media—Bekah and Ray have married, bought a house, advanced in their careers, and recently welcomed their daughter Madalyn Rae into the world. Here's their story, in Bekah's words:

"My 'Interracial' Engagement"

In 280 days, I get to marry my best friend—the man I admire more than anyone else in the world.

And some people are surprised he's black.

When Ray Holden and I started dating during my sophomore year, I don't think I fully understood racism. To me, it was an abstract—a deep feeling that people masked (sometimes successfully, sometimes not). But it was "out there," not something I experienced myself.

Now I have, at least to an extent.

When people see Ray and me together, the reactions are mixed. Sometimes we get warm smiles of approval. Other times we're snubbed and given sideways glances.

The first time I felt the disapproval of others stung. Suddenly, racism had a face. Sometimes the face was white, sometimes it was black. A coworker would ask me why I was dating a black guy. In public, Ray would hear a couple of random black men call him "white boy" as he and my family walked by.

But more times than not, people aren't unkind. They're just curious. Once, a girl was washing her hands beside me—a stranger who is now a very dear friend—and she just blurted out, "Hey, you're dating a black guy, right?" I laughed as I dried my hands. "Umm, yes, I am. And who are you?"

---

154 Rebekah Holden, "My 'Interracial' Engagement" in *The Collegian*, September 14, 2018. today. bju.edu/perspective/interracial-engagement. The fact that Ray and Bekah met at Bob Jones University—which banned interracial dating until March 4, 2000—makes Ray and Bekah's story all the more remarkable. Thankfully, BJU has repented of that sinful, shameful policy. Read the *New York Times* article about BJU's decision. nytimes.com/library/national/030400bobjones-edu.html.

Her question led to a wonderful conversation (not to mention a sweet friendship), and I was able to tell her our story. I love Ray for his person. I love that he surprised me on Labor Day by showing up to my 8 a.m. class with my favorite Starbucks drink. I love him for his character, for the way he treats other people, for his strength and his gentleness.

So, when it comes to our relationship and our commitment to each other, ethnicity just isn't a factor. Our faith is. His character is. In the most vital ways, because of our love for Christ and for each other, we're the same, not different.

I remember when I first learned this lesson. I was a teenager in Ohio, and my youth pastor, Joe Tyrpak, took our youth group on a mission exposure trip in Cleveland. We visited a mosque and a synagogue. We attended a Roman Catholic service and a liberal Protestant service (during which the female pastor celebrated homosexuality and denied the Trinity). The people in the Catholic church and the liberal church looked just like me—but we could not have been more different!

Our last visit was to a black Baptist church. Those people seemed so different from me in their appearance and expressiveness in worship. But they were joyful. They were welcoming. They were actually the only fellow believers we met during our tours. So they weren't different from us at all. They were the same. Because, as my dad says, "grace erases race."[155]

One of the most frequent questions I get asked is, "What do your parents think?" Usually I just tell them that race isn't a relevant factor in our family. My dad is actually the one who set us up, and my mom is thrilled that I'm going to marry a wonderful man who loves me, serves me and cares for me better than I deserve.

---

155   My statement that "grace erases race" requires some clarification. My son-in-law is black, not "transparent." Loving him means learning the story of African Americans and empathizing with the challenges he faces, as well as the triumphs. So race (ethnicity) still exists, and to claim to be "color blind" can actually be hurtful. Ray is *black*, Bekah is *white*, and they both bring to their marriage their beautiful and sometimes painful stories. What I intended to say by "grace erases race" is that our common experience as fallen creatures who bear God's image and as forgiven saints who cling to Christ makes our ethnic and cultural differences irrelevant, or at least manageable. Race is never truly erased. According to Revelation 5:9–10, we will always display our beautiful diversity, even in heaven. But Rebekah is right when she says that "race isn't a relevant factor in our family." That is "grace erases race" in a Galatians 3:28 way. I love Ray as my son. And we are *the same* in the ways that matter most.

I'm not crazy about the term "interracial dating" or "interracial marriage." We're both human (Acts 17:26). More importantly, we're both Christians (Galatians 3:27–28). And our ethnic differences are beautiful. Opposition can be challenging, but we work through it, and it brings us even closer together.

I couldn't be more excited to marry my best friend. And we're praying that our union will be a small example of the creativity of God and the barrier-breaking power of the Gospel.

CHAPTER 15

BIG-TENT ORTHODOXY FOR THE 21ST CENTURY

"Behold, how good and pleasant it is
when brothers dwell in unity!"

—*Psalm 133:1*

For the last several years I enjoyed working with a missions organization, Biblical Ministries Worldwide (BMW). BMW is passionate about helping churches plant "healthy churches everywhere." I enjoyed waving the banner for worldwide missions in American churches, colleges, conferences, and camps. And I enjoyed getting on the field, training Christian leaders in India, South Africa, Madagascar, Sweden, Palau, and beyond. BMW has over six hundred team members serving in more than sixty countries.

One thing I love about BMW is that it's an example of "big-tent" orthodoxy.

Here's what I mean. Last year I was with a group of twenty of our missionaries in Africa. We gathered from all over the continent for fellowship, preaching, and prayer. Despite our small number, we hailed from an astounding variety of backgrounds. Our little group had roots from Cedarville University, Tennessee Temple University, Liberty University, Baptist Bible College (later Clarks Summit University), Northland Baptist Bible College, Appalachian Bible College, Master's Seminary, Southeastern Baptist Theological Seminary, New Orleans Baptist Theological Seminary, Southwestern Baptist Theological Seminary, Grand Rapids Theological Seminary (now Cornerstone Seminary), Word of Life, Bob Jones University, and a sampling of African Bible institutes. The missionaries had been in the IFCA, the GARBC, and the SBC (including the IMB). Various members had trained with ACBC and Campus Crusade for Christ (now Cru). And that's in a group of twenty!

If I were to include other BMW missionaries, the list of institutions in their backgrounds would expand to include Moody Bible Institute, Pensacola Christian College, Faith Baptist Bible College, Clearwater Christian College, Calvary University, Calvary Baptist Theological Seminary, Shepherds Theological Seminary, Detroit Baptist Theological Seminary, Trinity Evangelical Divinity School, BIOLA, Veritas University, West Coast Baptist College, Piedmont International University (now Carolina University), and a bunch of state and international schools. And those missionaries are sent from and supported by *thousands* of churches!

So how does that work? How can this "menagerie of missionaries" from so many different places work together without infighting? Well, they don't always agree. They're human. But I attribute BMW's beautiful unity to two things. First, *BMW has a doctrinal statement that brings people together*—and that also excludes even faithful brothers and sisters who differ from what BMW believes. The group has converged around biblical orthodoxy, not an ever-expanding list of Christian cultural preferences.

Second, *BMW is on mission*. Literally. They're missionaries. They're working together to evangelize the lost, plant churches, disciple Christians, and train leaders. They're not waving other banners—whether of alma maters, past or present associations, or personal convictions. They're laboring together, within a clear doctrinal statement, for *gospel advance*.

As I've interacted with pastors around the United States and missionaries around the world, I regularly hear a yearning to be part of something bigger than themselves. Yes, they're hungry for fellowship. But they want more. They want collaboration for gospel purposes. They want to do something. They may or may not wish to be part of an official denomination. They may feel like ministry "misfits." But they're orthodox, they're intolerant of false teaching, and they're hungry for ministry mentors and partners. When they find pastors who are doctrinally and missionally aligned—be it in the GARBC, the IFCA, the SBC, or the Evangelical Free church—they find brothers in arms.

What I enjoyed about BMW wasn't some lowest-common-denominator unity that ignored important doctrinal differences. We celebrated a big tent of biblical and missional orthodoxy. And again, this is what early fundamentalism was all about—*unity* around core Bible doctrines and *deference* regarding personal preferences. More importantly, this is the kind of unity Scripture calls for, again and again and again. This smorgasbord of faithful Christians is "standing firm in one spirit, with one mind striving side by side for the faith of the gospel" (Philippians 1:27). Isn't that better than "biting and devouring and consuming one another" (Galatians 5:15)?

To some degree, these efforts are an example of what I believe is a much-needed work at realignment and reengagement. Starting with the last half of the twentieth century, some fundamentalists or conservatives began to have a truncated view of the universal church and its importance. As a result, they were too willing to break with legitimate brothers and sisters for illegitimate reasons. This was a sweeping change from the early fundamentalists who had united across denominational lines because they faced a common enemy. Those early fundamentalists didn't stop being Baptists, Presbyterians, or Methodists. But they reached over their denominational fences to lock arms on key issues. They had been backed into a corner by growing secularism, and they responded not only by writing some articles, but by planting the churches and building the ministries that we've enjoyed for the last century.

Christian unity must start in local churches, but it can't stay there. Jesus' prayer in John 17 wasn't just for one local church. It was for all His people—including all who would come to Him through the apostles' witness (John 17:20). It was for the church universal. It was for us. Jesus cared about the unity of His full-orbed, international, imperfect, sometimes-schismatic church. He prayed for it. Indeed, He *bled* for it.

Psalm 133 tells us that unity among God's people is *good*. When you've tasted it, is it not sweet? And when you've tasted schism, is it not bitter? Spurgeon writes,

> Christian unity is good in itself, good for ourselves, good for the brethren, good for our converts, good for the outside world; and for certain it is pleasant; for a loving heart must have pleasure and give pleasure in associating with others of like nature. A church united for

years in earnest service of the Lord is a well of goodness and joy to all those who dwell round about it.[156]

Because Christian unity is so precious to our Father, it should be so precious to His children. With an eye on the unity Jesus bled to achieve, I want to end the book with seven resolutions on unity in the truth for us to pursue together. May God help us to embrace and embody them.

1. RESOLVED: *To Repent of Our Schismatic Spirit and Actions*

The first step in the pursuit of peace is the confession of sinful division. When I had my "Diotrephes" moment in which I realized that I had contributed to spiritual schism, I needed to confess that sin to God. And in a few cases, I needed to confess that sin to those I had unjustly criticized and separated from, both to my right and to my left.

I'm not asking you to repent of *necessary* but grievous separation. The Bible calls us to cut off heretics and to cut out church members who refuse to turn from their sin. Don't apologize for exercising biblical separation. But if you've added to Scripture, separated over preferences, slandered brothers, split churches, opposed fellow laborers, or otherwise hindered Christ's work through your schismatic spirit, repent of it, thankful that Jesus' blood cleanses you and me from all of our sins (1 John 1:7).

2. RESOLVED: *To Renew Our Commitment to the Authority and Sufficiency of Scripture*

In calling for greater unity, I'm not arguing that we should lower the bar regarding obedience to Scripture. Quite the opposite. I'm pleading with my brothers and sisters to put Scripture *back in its rightful place*, far above our traditions and preferences.

What distinguishes evangelicals throughout history is not our standards, our dress codes, or our other idiosyncrasies. At our best, we are *people of the Book*. We read it, memorize it, meditate on it, preach it, pray it, defend it, and seek to conscientiously obey it. We love the Bible—so much so that we wouldn't dare to delete any of it, and so much so that we wouldn't dare to supplement it.

---

156   C. H. Spurgeon, *The Treasury of David* (Peabody, MA: Hendrickson Publishers, 1988), 3:168.

I'm urging churches, mission boards, and colleges to renew their commitment to the inerrancy, authority, and sufficiency of Scripture. And I'm urging individual Christians—like you, reader, and like me—to admit when our appetite for Scripture has waned, leading to our spiritual malnourishment.

3. RESOLVED: *To Unite around Creeds, Not Arbitrary Extras*

One key way to promote unity is to follow the example of early fundamentalists: Identify a core of essential doctrines, then require agreement as a condition of Christian cooperation. This "credal" approach to ministry partnerships has worked for the church for two millennia, and it has been championed in our day by leaders like Carl Trueman.[157]

My burden here is twofold. First, while we are biblicists, church history has repeatedly taught us that it is necessary to have a robust and carefully worded doctrinal statement that states the truth so specifically that it can be affirmed or denied, but not merely dodged. To say with conviction, "This is what we believe"—and to be willing to break fellowship over it—is essential.[158]

But second, a sound doctrinal statement—whether original or traditional—hinders our temptation to keep adding new, arbitrary litmus tests for fellowship. A creed allows a church or ministry to say, "We require this—no less and no more."

Put another way, when we *minimize* a creed's importance, we drift toward liberalism. But when *supplement* a creed with unspoken extras, we drift toward legalism. Both alternatives are disastrous.

---

157 Carl Trueman, *Crisis of Confidence: Reclaiming the Historic Faith in a Culture Consumed with Individualism and Identity* (Wheaton, IL: Crossway, 2024).

158 The recoveries of Southern Baptist Theological Seminary under Al Mohler and Cedarville University under Thomas White were both achieved by the courageous enforcement of the institutions' creeds and the dismissal of faculty members who couldn't legitimately sign and teach the creeds. Trueman writes, "Creeds and confessions establish boundaries of belonging and, by implication, of exclusion. Both are necessary if the church is to have a meaningful corporate identity and unity." Trueman, 169. While Trueman argues in favor of ancient creeds, Grudem makes a strong case for updating creeds to address new heresies. Grudem, "When, Why, and For What?"

4. RESOLVED: *To Love Jesus' People As Jesus Commanded*

This may seem like a sentimental follow-up to Scripture and creed. But there is nothing sentimental about biblical love. Among the New Testament's barrage of love commands, 1 John 4:11 states, "Beloved, if God so loved us, we also ought to love one another." Love is what our Father dispenses to us and desires of us. *We are never more like the Triune God than when we love one another—especially when others don't deserve it.*

Matthew Henry writes,

> Divine love to the brethren should constrain ours…. This should be an invincible argument. The example of God should press us. We should be followers (or imitators) of him, as his dear children. The objects of the divine love should be the objects of ours. Shall we refuse to love those whom the eternal God hath loved?[159]

God is love, and He extends His love to the most undeserving. If we would be like Him, love is a crucial starting point. Our loveless and exacting criticism of other believers is unworthy of God and an abuse of the body of Christ.

5. RESOLVED: *To Pursue Peace and Peacemaking with Fellow Christians*

Scripture repeatedly urges God's people to *seek* and *pursue* and *strive for* peace (Romans 14:19; 1 Peter 3:11; Hebrews 12:14). Our Savior put a blessing on the heads of peacemakers, calling them "the sons of God" for participation in His own peacemaking work (Matthew 5:9). Paul tells us to allow the peace of Christ—and not our own schismatic natures—to rule us, personally and corporately (Colossians 3:15).

Puritan Jeremiah Burroughs closes his book on Christian unity with a chapter on the beauty of peace within Christ's church. Here is the book's final sentence: "Let us all study peace, seek peace, follow peace, pursue peace, and the God of peace be with us."[160]

---

159   Matthew Henry, *Matthew Henry's Commentary on the Whole Bible: Complete and Unabridged in One Volume* (Peabody, MA: Hendrickson Publishers, 1994), 2451.

160   Burroughs, 436.

Sadly, there are times when peace is impossible. We dare not say "peace, peace" when confronted with apostasy (Jeremiah 6:14; 8:11). Nor is peace always desired by others (Romans 12:18). "Some men," Alfred Pennyworth tells us, "just want to watch the world burn." But we will not be among them. We will pursue peace.

6. RESOLVED: *To Seek Fellowship with Orthodox Brothers and Sisters Outside of Our Circles*

Early fundamentalism was a sort of "evangelical ecumenism." And I long for that to return. Not tolerating unorthodoxy, of course. Not softening our commitment to the Scriptures. Not opening our arms to those who embrace a false gospel—whether they be Catholics, Methodists, or Baptists. But fostering a mutual appreciation for those who are committed to the same faith and same Lord we are, along with a mutual desire for cooperation where it is feasible in light of our doctrinal distinctives. There's an itch for this. I hear it all the time. Even those who are rightly protective of local church autonomy want to be part of community and collaboration broader than their individual churches.

The skeptic in me says there can be no real unity beyond church walls or denominational structures. But the church historian in me—and the *optimist* in me!—says that's not the case.

While unity must *begin within the local church*, the history of Christ's church shows the benefits of big-tent cooperation that *extends beyond the local church*. First-century churches helped meet each other's financial needs in hard times. Church councils resolved vital doctrinal disputes in the fourth and fifth centuries. The early fundamentalists labored together in the early twentieth century. And the eighteenth, nineteenth, and twentieth centuries demonstrated what Bible-believing Christians of various stripes can accomplish together—from Bible conferences to Bible colleges and seminaries, from mission boards to Bible societies, from publishing houses to radio stations, from military and college ministries to children's ministries, from Christian camps to rescue missions, and on and on it goes.

The fact is, despite our sinfulness and independence, we *have* managed to collaborate for gospel advance in the past. Can we not do so in the future?

Mark Dever has been a bold voice calling for (and practicing) sacrificial fellowship outside of his own "group." He poses a series of provocative questions for churches to consider:

> Do you happily give away your best players to other churches? Do you rejoice if, after praying for revival, revival comes to the church down the street? . . . Do you pray regularly for the church down the street as well as the other churches in your city? Do you give any portion of your budget to revitalizing old or raising up new churches in your city, around the nation, or abroad?

He then offers a pull-no-punches critique of the schismatic attitude which prevails in most churches:

> Too often, a grotesque competitiveness between churches marks evangelical churches. But a Great Commission church does not compete with other gospel-preaching churches because it knows every gospel-preaching church *is playing for the same team*.[161]

Broadening your fellowship can begin with a baby step. Pray for an orthodox, gospel-preaching church other than your own each Sunday—including those from other denominations. Swap preachers with a like-minded church in your area for a Sunday morning. Have a combined Thanksgiving service with Bible-believing churches in your region. Get out of your spiritual silo.

7. RESOLVED: *To Unite for Great-Commission Work with Renewed Urgency*

Christian unity strengthens Christian witness. Our goal isn't to get along so we can enjoy potlucks, put on conferences, produce Christian movies, and flex our political muscles. Our goals are much, *much* bigger!

As we've learned from Philippians 1:27, John 13:35, and John 17:21, gospel advance can grind to a halt when gospel workers are at each other's throats. There's a reason why many missionaries look at the infighting of American Christians with confusion and disgust. When you're working to spread the gospel in the world's darkest places, you don't fight over music styles, Bible versions, or degrees of Calvinism. You rejoice to meet a brother in Christ—*any* brother in Christ—even if you can't plant a church together.

---

161   Mark Dever, *Understanding the Great Commission* (Nashville, TN: B&H Publishing Group, 2016), 33–34.

Were we consumed with the Great Commission, we would be less inclined to fight other believers. It is my prayer that Christians would respond to potential skirmishes the way Nehemiah blew off Sanballat and Tobiah: "I am doing a great work and I cannot come down. Why should the work stop while I leave it and come down to you?" (Nehemiah 6:3). Let's get back on mission, together.

When I was in college, classmates and I were regularly reminded of the needs of the lost. We would recite a brief axiom each day in chapel: "The most sobering reality in the world today is that people are dying and going to hell today." As I see conservative Christians emphasizing the wrong things, I'm tempted to post a series of satirical memes online: "The most sobering reality in the world today is that Christian ladies are wearing shorts today…that churches are using praise bands today…that Christians are getting tattoos today." It's silly. But it's also deadly serious. Our stubborn insistence to "major on the minors"—and even divide from good brothers over these things!—is maddening. Especially when, moment by moment, people really *are* dying and going to hell today.

Conclusion: Bottom-Line Motives for Unity

We've spent a lot of time discussing when division is necessary and when division is sinful. We need to become experts at distinguishing between biblical separation and fleshly schism.

But let me boil things down as we wrap things up. Why is it so essential that we pursue peace with other Bible-believing Christians?

> *Because God commands it.*
> *Because Jesus prayed for it.*
> *Because the body needs it.*
> *Because the world is watching.*
> *Because the world is perishing.*
> *Because Jesus bled for it.*

"By this all people will know that you are my disciples,

if you have love for one another."

—*John 13:35*

"…that they may be one, even as we are one…

so that the world may believe

that you have sent me."

—*John 17:11, 21*

BIBLIOGRAPHY

Adams, Isaac. *Talking About Race: Gospel Hope for Hard Conversations*. Grand Rapids, MI: Zondervan Reflective, 2022.

Anderson, Chris. "Grace to You, Mom!" In *Gospel Meditations for Mothers*. Edited by Chris Anderson. Grayson, GA: Church Works Media, 2018.

Anyabwile, Thabiti. "Bearing the Image: Identity, the Work of Christ, and the Church." https://t4g.org/resources/thabiti-anyabwile/bearing-the-image-identity-the-work-of-christ-and-the-church-session-ii.

Armstrong, John H., ed. *The Coming Evangelical Crisis: Current Challenges to the Authority of Scripture and the Gospel*. Chicago, IL: Moody Press, 1996.

Ashbrook, John E. *The New Neutralism II: Exposing the Gray of Compromise*. Mentor, OH: Here I Stand Books, 1992.

Bargas, Richard P., ed. *Fight the Good Fight: Reclaiming Biblical Fundamentalism*. Grand Rapids, MI: IFCA Press, 2024.

Barrett, Michael P. V. *The Beauty of Holiness: A Guide to Biblical Worship*. Greenville, SC: Ambassador International, 2006.

Baucham, Voddie T., Jr. *Fault Lines: The Social Justice Movement and Evangelicalism's Looming Catastrophe*. Washington, D.C.: Salem Books, 2021.

Bauder, Kevin T. "Exhortation to 2006 Graduating Students." Preached at Puritan Reformed Theological Seminary. https://tinysa.com/sermon/620619053.

———. "Fundamentalism." In *Four Views on the Spectrum of Evangelicalism*. Edited by Andrew David Naselli and Collin Hansen. Grand Rapids, MI: Zondervan, 2011.

———. "What's That You Smell?" In *Pilgrims on the Sawdust Trail: Evangelical Ecumenism and the Quest for Christian Identity*. Edited by Timothy George. Grand Rapids, MI: Baker, 2004.

Bauder, Kevin T., and Robert Delnay. *One in Hope and Doctrine: Origins of Baptist Fundamentalism (1870-1950)*. Schaumburg, IL: Regular Baptist Books, 2014.

Beale, David O. *In Pursuit of Purity: American Fundamentalism Since 1850*. Greenville, SC: Bob Jones University Press, 1986.

———. *SBC: House on the Sand?* Greenville, SC: Bob Jones University Press, 1985.

Berg, Jim. *Essential Virtues: Marks of the Christ-Centered Life*. Greenville, SC: JourneyForth, 2008.

Billheimer, Paul E. *Love Covers: A Biblical Design for Unity in the Body of Christ*. Minneapolis, MN: Bethany House Publishers, 1981.

Binning, Hugh. *A Treatise on Christian Love: With an Extract from The Sinner's Sanctuary*. Carlisle, PA: Banner of Truth Trust, 2009.

Bixby, Don W. "Separation in Search of Balance." Class paper at Central Baptist Theological Seminary, 1990.

Blomberg, Craig L. *From Pentecost to Patmos*. Nashville, TN: B&H Academic, 2006.

Boice, James Montgomery, and Benjamin E. Sasse, eds. *Here We Stand! A Call from Confessing Evangelicals for a Modern Reformation*. Phillipsburg, NJ: P&R Publishing, 1996.

Brooks, Thomas. *Precious Remedies Against Satan's Devices* in *The Works of Thomas Brooks*. Edited by Alexander B. Grosart. Carlisle, PA: The Banner of Truth Trust, 2001.

Bruce, A. B. *The Training of the Twelve*. Grand Rapids, MI: Kregel Publications, 1988.

Burroughs, Jeremiah. *Irenicum to the Lovers of Truth and Peace*. Edited by Don Kistler. Morgan, PA: Soli Deo Gloria Publications, 1997.

Carson, D. A. *Love in Hard Places*. Wheaton, IL: Crossway Books, 2002.

———. *The Cross and Christian Ministry: Leadership Lessons from 1 Corinthians*. Grand Rapids, MI: Baker Books, 1993.

———. *The Difficult Doctrine of the Love of God*. Wheaton, IL: Crossway Books, 2000.

Chan, Francis. *Until Unity*. Colorado Springs, CO: David C. Cook, 2021.

Clowney, Edmund P. *The Church.* Downers Grove, IL: InterVarsity Press, 1995.

Compton, R. Bruce. "2 Thessalonians 3:6-15 and Biblical Separation." *The Sentinel.* Fall 1988.

Crowley, J. D. "Check It Off the List." In *Gospel Meditations for Missions.* Edited by Chris Anderson. Grayson, GA: Church Works Media, 2011.

Davenant, John. *An Exhortation to Brotherly Communion Betwixt the Protestant Churches.* Originally published in London in 1641. Published online by the University of Michigan. https://quod.lib. umich.edu/e/eebo2/A37175.0001.001.

Deets, David. "Defending Orthodox Doctrine: A Call to Arms." *Fight the Good Fight: Reclaiming Biblical Fundamentalism.* Edited by Richard P. Bargas. Grand Rapids, MI: IFCA Press, 2024.

Dever, Mark. *Nine Marks of a Healthy Church.* Wheaton, IL: Crossway Books, 2004.

———. *The Church: The Gospel Made Visible.* Nashville: B&H, 2012.

———. *Understanding the Great Commission.* Nashville, TN: B&H Publishing Group, 2016.

Dever, Mark, and Paul Alexander. *The Deliberate Church: Building Your Ministry on the Gospel.* Wheaton, IL: Crossway Books, 2005.

DeYmaz, Mark. *Building a Healthy Multi-Ethnic Church: Mandate, Commitments, and Practices of a Diverse Congregation.* Hoboken, NJ: Jossey-Bass, 2007.

DeYoung, Kevin. *The Hole in Our Holiness: Filling the Gap Between Gospel Passion and the Pursuit of Godliness.* Wheaton, IL: Crossway, 2012.

Doran, David M. *For the Sake of His Name: Challenging a New Generation for World Missions.* Allen Park, MI: Student Global Impact, 2002.

Frame, John M. *Contemporary Worship Music: A Biblical Defense.* Phillipsburg, PA: P&R Publishing, 1997.

———. *Worship in Spirit and Truth: A Refreshing Study of the Principles and Practice of Biblical Worship.* Phillipsburg, PA: P&R Publishing, 1996.

Garland, David E. *Baker Exegetical Commentary on the New Testament: 1 Corinthians.* Grand Rapids, MI: Baker Academic, 2003.

Glover, Robert Hall. *The Bible Basis of Missions.* Chicago, IL: Moody Press, 1946.

Gregory, Richard I. and Richard W. Gregory. *On the Level: Discovering the Levels of Biblical Relationships Among Believers*. Grandville, MI: IFCA Press, 2005.

Grudem, Wayne. "When, Why, and For What Should We Draw New Boundaries?" *Beyond the Bounds: Open Theism and the Undermining of Biblical Christianity*. Edited by John Piper, Justin Taylor, and Paul Kjoss Helseth. Wheaton, IL: Crossway, 2003.

Hansen, Collin. "Introduction." *Four Views on the Spectrum of Evangelicalism*. Edited by Andrew David Naselli and Collin Hansen. Grand Rapids, MI: Zondervan, 2011.

Harris, Richard A. "A Plea for Christian Statesmanship." *The Challenge*. December 1997.

Hendriksen, William. *New Testament Commentary: Exposition of Ephesians*. Grand Rapids, MI: Baker Academic, 2007.

Henry, Carl F. H, ed. *Fundamentals of the Faith*. Grand Rapids, MI: Baker Book House, 1969.

Henry, Matthew. *Matthew Henry's Commentary on the Whole Bible: Complete and Unabridged in One Volume*. Peabody, MA: Hendrickson Publishers, 1991.

Hodge, Charles. *Commentary on the Epistle to the Romans*. Grand Rapids, MI: William B. Eerdmans Publishing Company, 1994.

Holden, Rebekah. "My 'Interracial' Engagement." *The Collegian*, September 14, 2018. https://today.bju.edu/perspective/interracial-engagement.

Jamieson, Robert, A. R. Fausset, and David Brown. *A Commentary Critical and Explanatory on the Old and New Testaments*. Grand Rapids, MI: Zondervan Publishing House, 1999.

Jeffers, James. S. *The Greco-Roman World of the New Testament Era*. Downers Grove, IL: IVP Academic, 1999.

Johnson, Phil. "Dead Right: The Failure of Fundamentalism." https://www.thegracelifepulpit.com/pdf/deadright_.pdf.

Jones, Bob, Jr. *Fundamentals of Faith*. Greenville, SC: Bob Jones University Press, 1962.

Keller, Tim. *The Prodigal God: Recovering the Heart of the Christian Faith*. New York, NY: Dutton, 2008.

Kennedy, John F. *Profiles in Courage*. New York: HarperCollins, 2003.

King, Martin Luther, Jr. "Meet the Press," April 17, 1960. https://www.youtube.com/watch?v=1q881g1L_d8&t=33s.

Kuiper, R. B. *The Glorious Body of Christ: A Scriptural Appreciation of the One Holy Church.* Edinburgh: Banner of Truth, 1967.

Lightfoot, J. B. *St. Paul's Epistle to the Galatians.* Peabody, MA: Hendrickson Publishers, 1993.

Linne, Shai. *The New Reformation: Finding Hope in the Fight for Ethnic Unity.* Chicago, IL: Moody Publishers, 2021.

Lloyd-Jones, D. Martin. "Evangelical Unity." https://www.mljtrust.org/sermons/itinerant-preaching/evangelical-unity.

———. *Knowing the Times: Addresses Delivered on Various Occasions 1942-77.* Edinburgh: Banner of Truth, 1989.

Luther, Martin. *Luther's Works.* Volume 25. Edited by Hilton C. Oswald. St. Louis, MO: Concordia, 1972.

Lutzer, Erwin W. *Why the Cross Can Do What Politics Can't: When They See You, Do They See Jesus?* Eugene, OR: Harvest House Publishers, 1999.

MacArthur, John. *The Body Dynamic: Finding Where You Fit in Today's Church.* Colorado Springs, CO: Chariot Victor Publishing, 1996.

———. *The MacArthur New Testament Commentary: 1-3 John.* Chicago, IL: Moody Publishers, 2007.

———. *The Truth War: Fighting for Certainty in an Age of Deception.* Nashville, TN: Thomas Nelson, 2007.

Machen, J. Gresham. "Are We Schismatics?" *Presbyterian Guardian,* April 20, 1936, 22.

———. *Christianity and Liberalism.* Grand Rapids, MI: William B. Eerdmans Publishing Company, 2009.

Mack, Wayne A. and David Swavely. *Life in the Father's House: A Member's Guide to the Local Church.* Phillipsburg, NJ: P&R Publishing, 1996.

Maclaren, Alexander. *The Acts of the Apostles.* Grand Rapids, MI: Zondervan Publishing House, 1959.

Marsden, George M. *Fundamentalism and American Culture: The Shaping of Twentieth Century Evangelicalism: 1870-1925.* New York, NY: Oxford University Press, 1980.

———. *Reforming Fundamentalism: Fuller Seminary and the New Evangelicalism*. Grand Rapids, MI: William B. Eerdmans Publishing Company, 1987.

Mbewe, Conrad. *Unity: Striving Side by Side for the Gospel*. Wheaton, IL: Crossway, 2024.

McCune, Rolland. *Ecclesiastical Separation*. Detroit, MI: Detroit Baptist Theological Seminary, n.d.

———. *Promise Unfulfilled: The Failed Strategy of Modern Evangelicalism*. Greenville, SC: Ambassador International, 2004.

McLachlan, Douglas R. *Reclaiming Authentic Fundamentalism*. Independence, MO: American Association of Christian Schools, 1993.

Mitchell, Curtis. *God in the Garden: The Story of the Billy Graham New York Crusade*. Garden City, NY: Doubleday & Company, Inc., 1957.

Mitchell, Margaret M. *Paul and the Rhetoric of Reconciliation: An Exegetical Investigation*. Louisville, KY: Westminster/John Knox Press, 1993.

Mohler, R. Albert. "A Call for Theological Triage and Christian Maturity." July 12, 2005. https://albertmohler.com/2005/07/12/a-call-for-theological-triage-and-christian-maturity/.

———. "Confessional Evangelicalism." *Four Views on the Spectrum of Evangelicalism*. Edited by Andrew David Naselli and Collin Hansen. Grand Rapids, MI: Zondervan, 2011.

———. "Well, That Didn't Take Long." *World Magazine*, May 2, 2024. https://wng.org/opinions/well-that-didnt-take-long-1714647569.

Moritz, Fred. *"Be Ye Holy": The Call to Christian Separation*. Greenville, SC: Bob Jones University Press, 1994.

———. *Contending for the Faith*. Greenville, SC: Bob Jones University Press, 2000.

Morris, Leon. *Galatians: Paul's Charter of Christian Freedom*. Downers Grove, IL: IVP Academic, 1996.

Mounce, Robert H. *Romans*. Nashville, TN: B&H, 1995.

Murray, Iain H. *Evangelicalism Divided: A Record of Crucial Change in the Years 1950 to 2000*. Carlisle, PA: The Banner of Truth Trust, 2000.

———. *Martyn Lloyd-Jones: Letters 1919-1981*. Carlisle, PA: The Banner of Truth Trust, 1994.

Naselli, Andrew David and Collin Hansen, eds. *Four Views on the Spectrum of Evangelicalism*. Grand Rapids, MI: Zondervan, 2011.

Naselli, Andrew David and J. D. Crowley. *Conscience: What It Is, How to Train It, and Loving Those Who Differ*. Wheaton, IL: Crossway, 2016.

Nutz, Earl. "The Gospel of Grace (Galatians 2)." *Biblical Viewpoint: Focus on Galatians* 31 (1997).

Ortiz, Manuel. *One New People: Models for Developing a Multiethnic Church*. Downers Grove, IL: IVP Academic, 1996.

Ortlund, Gavin. *Finding the Right Hills to Die On: The Case for Theological Triage*. Wheaton, IL: Crossway, 2020.

Owen, John. *The Mortification of Sin*. Fearn, Ross-shire, UK: Christian Focus, 1996.

———. *The Works of John Owen*. Volume XIII. Edited by William H. Gould. Carlisle, PA: The Banner of Truth Trust, 1967.

Packer, J. I. *"Fundamentalism" and the Word of God: Some Evangelical Principles*. Grand Rapids, MI: William B. Eerdmans Publishing Co., 1972.

Panosian, Edward M. "John Knox: The Thundering Scot." *Faith of Our Fathers: Scenes from Church History*. Edited by Mark Sidwell. Greenville, SC: Bob Jones University Press, 1989.

Pickering, Ernest. *Biblical Separation: The Struggle for a Pure Church*. Schaumburg, IL: Regular Baptist Press, 1995.

———. *The Tragedy of Compromise: The Origin and Impact of New Evangelicalism*. Greenville, SC: Bob Jones University Press, 1994.

Piper, John. *Bloodlines: Race, Cross, and the Christian*. Wheaton, IL: Crossway, 2011.

———. *Let the Nations Be Glad! The Supremacy of God in Missions*. Grand Rapids, MI: Baker Books, 1993.

Plumer, William S. *Psalms: A Critical and Expository Commentary with Doctrinal and Practical Remarks*. Carlisle, PA: The Banner of Truth Trust, 2016.

Rice, John R. *Come Out—Or Stay In?* Nashville, TN: Thomas Nelson Inc., 1974.

Ross, Allen P. *Recalling the Hope of Glory: Biblical Worship from the Garden to the New Creation*. Grand Rapids: Kregel, 2006.

Ryken, Philip Graham. *City on a Hill: Reclaiming the Biblical Pattern for the Church in the 21ˢᵗ Century.* Chicago, IL: Moody Publishers, 2003.

———. *Galatians.* Phillipsburg, NJ: P & R Publishing, 2005.

Ryle, J. C. *Expository Thoughts on the Gospels: John 10:31 – John 21:25.* Grand Rapids, MI: Baker Book House, 2007.

———. *Holiness: Its Nature, Hindrances, Difficulties, and Roots.* Darlington, England: Evangelical Press, 1999.

Schaeffer, Francis A. *The Great Evangelical Disaster.* Wheaton, IL: Crossway, 1984.

———. *The Mark of a Christian.* Downers Grove, IL: InterVarsity Press, 2006.

Schaff, Philip. *History of the Christian Church.* Volume VII. Grand Rapids, MI: Wm. B. Eerdmans Publishing Company, 1910.

Schreiner, Thomas R. *Romans.* Grand Rapids, MI: Baker Books, 1998.

Sidwell, Mark. *The Dividing Line: Understanding and Applying Biblical Separation.* Greenville, SC: Bob Jones University Press, 1998.

Singleton, James E. "Tensions Between Older and Younger Fundamentalists!" *Whetstone.* May 25, 2023.

Snoeberger, Mark. "Is Ethics Ever a Matter of Indifference?" Detroit Baptist Theological Seminary blog, April 29, 2024. https://dbts.edu/2024/04/29/is-ethics-ever-a-matter-of-indifference.

Spurgeon, Charles Haddon. *The Metropolitan Tabernacle Pulpit.* Volume V. London: Passmore & Alabaster, 1879.

———. *The Sword and the Trowel.* January 1865.

———. *The Sword and the Trowel.* November 1887.

———. *The Treasury of David.* Peabody, MA: Hendrickson Publishers, 1988.

———. "Unity in Christ." In *The Complete Works of C. H. Spurgeon.* Volume 12. Cleveland, OH: Pilgrim, 2013.

Stott, John R. W. *The Letters of John: An Introduction and Commentary.* Grand Rapids, MI: William B. Eerdmans Publishing Co., 1988.

———. *The Message of Galatians: Only One Way.* Downers Grove, IL: IVP Academic, 1968.

Swindoll, Charles R. *The Church Awakening: An Urgent Call for Renewal.* New York, NY: FaithWords, 2010.

Taylor, Dean H. *The Thriving Church: The True Measure of Growth.* Greenville, SC: JourneyForth, 2019.

Taylor, Justin. "Levels of Doctrine." The Gospel Coalition, March 17, 2010. https://www.thegospelcoalition.org/blogs/justin-taylor/how-do-you-evaluate-and-weigh-the-importance-of-various-doctrines/.

Tetreau, Joel. *Three Lines in the Evangelical Sand: Type A, B, C Fundamentalism.* Pre-publication copy.

Thiessen, Henry Clarence. *Introduction to the New Testament.* Grand Rapids, MI: Wm. B. Eerdmans Publishing Company, 1943.

Thomas, Derek. *Let's Study Galatians.* Carlisle, PA: Banner of Truth Trust, 2004.

Torrey, Reuben A., ed. *The Fundamentals: A Testimony to the Truth.* Grand Rapids, MI: Baker Books, 1998 reprint.

Trueman, Carl. *Crisis of Confidence: Reclaiming the Historic Faith in a Culture Consumed with Individualism and Identity.* Wheaton, IL: Crossway, 2024.

Van Gelderen, John. "The Fallacy of the Slippery Slope." *Revival Focus.* September 5, 2004. https://www.revivalfocus.org/the-fallacy-of-the-slippery-slope.

Wells, David. *The Courage to Be Protestant: Truth-lovers, Marketers, and Emergents in the Postmodern World.* Grand Rapids, MI: William B. Eerdmans Publishing Company, 2008.

Wilson, Jared. *The Imperfect Disciple: Grace For People Who Can't Get Their Act Together.* Grand Rapids, MI: Baker Books, 2017.

The
SCANDAL
of
SCHISM

STUDY QUESTIONS
FOR DISCUSSION

Chapter 1: The Lay of the Land

1. Why is the history in this chapter important for all Christians to understand, not just pastors and seminary students?

2. How can you pursue biblical holiness without falling into unbiblical asceticism?

3. Why is "contending for the faith" (Jude 3) essential? When is it necessary to defend the faith instead of showing deference?

Chapter 2: He Takes a Good Stand

1. Discuss the differences between biblical separation and unbiblical schism. Why is understanding this distinction critical for Christians?

2. How has cooperation or schism in the body of Christ affected you personally?

3. What are some elements of a schismatic approach to separation? As you reflect on this chapter, are any of these elements present in your life now or in your experience?

Chapter 3: The Awakened Conscience of a Spiritual Misfit

1. Consider your approach to Christian unity. Are you more of an "on/off" switch or a "dimmer"?

2. How does the phrase, "unity doesn't require unanimity" help your understanding of both the need for and beauty of diversity within the body of Christ?

3. What criteria does this chapter mention as reasons for biblical separation? How do these help clarify your approach to the issue of separation?

4. How can churches avoid a spirit of judgmentalism and division while acknowledging legitimate differences within the broader Christian community?

Chapter 4: Good Medicine: Antidotes to the Scandal of Schism

1. How does the gospel motivate us and enable us to overcome personal divisions?

2. Can you identify any area of your life where you have subtly embraced legalism as a means to godliness?

3. How can grace, both experienced and extended, change how you think about sanctification?

4. How does a commitment to the Great Commission cultivate a deeper unity within a church?

5. Are there any areas of your Christian life where you have elevated personal convictions and standards to the level of Scripture?

Chapter 5: Scripture Commands Separation from False Teachers

1. Why is it so dangerous to minimize heresy for the sake of evangelism?

2. Why is it important for a church to first fight, not flee, when confronted with false teaching?

3. What are some ways you can be better equipped to identify and biblically respond to false teaching?

4. Are you convinced that separation from false teachers is a biblical mandate? How has this chapter refocused or encouraged you?

Chapter 6: Scripture Commands Separation from Unrepentant Christians

1. Have you ever had to distance yourself from someone due to their unrepentant lifestyle? How did it affect you?

2. What is the ultimate goal of church discipline?

3. What are some of the reasons that church discipline is essential when a church member is unrepentant?

4. Practically, how does a Christian suspend normal relationships until repentance is evident?

Chapter 7: Jesus' Passion for Loving Unity

1. What extremes do we need to avoid in a pursuit of a "pure unity" and a "unified purity"?

2. Why are love and unity as critical to Christianity as sound doctrine?

3. Do you see any potential barriers to loving unity in your local church? How can you contribute to loving unity as a member or as a church leader?

4. How does the doctrine of the Trinity practically affect your commitment to truth, love, and unity?

Chapter 8: Diotrephes and Schismatic Ambition

1. Based on the teaching in 2 John and 3 John, how can we distinguish between separation, cooperation, and schism?

2. How would you describe the underlying motivation of Diotrephes? Why is this spirit so dangerous in a church?

3. Do you recognize any schismatic ambition in your own heart?

Chapter 9: Peter and the Fear of Man

1. Describe Peter's actions and how they confused the gospel.

2. What motivated Paul to confront Peter so sternly?

3. How does biblical separation protect the gospel? How does illegitimate or un-biblical separation undermine the gospel?

4. What are some ways to deal with the fear of man that can lead to a schismatic spirit?

Chapter 10: The Holy Corinthian Mess

1. How do Paul's commendations of the Corinthian church change your view of other "messy" Christians or churches?

2. Why should we value *every* gospel-preaching church?

3. How does the image of the church as a body encourage you to pursue healing and promote unity where there are divisions within your church?

Chapter 11: Worship Is Not a War

1. How should the doctrine of the sufficiency of Scripture inform your understanding of worship?

2. How can worship music foster unity instead of causing division?

3. Do you find it difficult to appreciate the music of other church members? What would it require for you to stretch yourself in being "willing to sing one another's music"?

4. How can you help to resolve any conflicts about worship styles and practices in your church?

Chapter 12: The Most Essential Unity: The Local Church

1. "Unity is built on the gospel—not the gospel-plus." What are some "gospel-plus" areas that Christians and churches may be tempted to unite around? Why is the gospel the only legitimate unifier?

2. Based on Ephesians 4:1-6, how can church members experience and contribute to unity?

3. Why is fostering unity a significant responsibility for church leaders? How do the qualifications for pastors and deacons highlight this?

4. What is the ultimate goal of unity?

Chapter 13: The Forgotten Virtue of Deference

1. What does deference mean? And what does deference *not* mean?

2. What principles in Romans 14 help promote deference within a local church?

3. How do differences within a congregation lead us to glorify God?

4. How does an understanding of categorized issues—core doctrines, important doctrines, and peripheral issues—help promote both unity and purity within a church?

Chapter 14: Racial Schism and America's Most Segregated Hour

1. What are some faulty ways of thinking about the human race that contribute to racism?

2. "A church that reaches its community will reflect its community." What are some changes your church can make to reach the *whole* community around you?

3. Read Ephesians 2 and describe the vertical and horizontal reconciliation accomplished by Christ.

4. What are some practical things you can do in your daily life to display the power of the gospel to heal racial divides?

Chapter 15: Big-Tent Orthodoxy for the 21st Century

1. What are the dangers of minimizing or supplementing a creed with unspoken extras?

2. How is biblical love different from sentimental feelings? How can recognizing that difference promote true unity in a church?

3. What are some practical steps you can take to grow in fellowship with brothers and sisters outside your "circles"?

4. How does focusing on eternal realities strengthen unity in the church? How can you support and participate in Great Commission efforts?

TOPIC INDEX

C

Calvary Baptist Theological Seminary, 178

Calvary University, 178

Calvinism, Calvinist(ic), 14, 40, 45, 159, 184

Campus Crusade for Christ, 178

Card, Michael, 125

cardplaying, 30

Carolina University, 178

Carson, D. A., 90, 111, 116, 121, 190

Catholic(s), Catholicism, 56, 67, 70, 71, 174, 183

Cedarville University, 177, 181

cessationism, cessationist(s), 44, 159

Chan, Francis, 90, 91, 190

church discipline, 30, 76, 77, 79, 83, 84, 122, 202

church polity, 26, 44, 45, 85, 159

CityAlight, 132

Clarks Summit University, 177

Claudius, 152

Clearwater Christian College, 178

Clowney, Edmund, 93, 190

Collier, Ken, 144

complementarianism, 159

compromise(d), compromising, 14, 26, 28, 29, 33, 38, 40, 45, 47, 49, 52, 94, 116, 189, 195

Compton, R. Bruce, 83, 191

Congregational(ists), 26, 45

Contemporary Christian Music (CCM), 38, 130, 134, 141, 191

continuationism, 159

Corinth, Corinthian(s), 80, 81, 82, 115, 116, 117, 118, 119, 120, 121, 122, 204

Cornelius, 110

Cornerstone Seminary, 177

covenant theology, 44, 159

creed(s), 23, 25, 158, 181, 182, 206

Critical Race Theory, 165

Crowley, J. D., 134, 166, 191, 195

Cyprus, 168

D

dancing, 30, 52, 129, 131, 132

Darwin, Charles, 22

Davenant, John, 25, 191

deacon(s), 115, 144, 145, 146, 148, 164, 204

Deets, David, 30, 191

Delnay, Robert, 45, 190

Demetrius, 103

Detroit Baptist Theological Seminary, 178

Dever, Mark, 29, 46, 76, 77, 137, 146, 184, 191

DeYmaz, Mark, 170, 190

Diotrephes, 14, 99, 102, 103, 104, 180, 203

dispensationalism, 159

diversity, 134, 152, 156, 161, 163, 164, 165, 168, 169, 171, 174, 200

division(s), divisive, 9, 10, 13, 21, 26, 30, 35, 39, 47,50, 58, 59, 79, 80, 84, 93, 103, 115, 116, 120, 125, 137, 163, 164, 170, 180, 185, 200, 201, 204

Dobras, Allan, 73

Downgrade Controversy, 69

dress, clothing, 29, 32, 50, 53, 55, 180

Duncan, Ligon, 46, 165

E

ecumenism, 47, 75, 94, 183

egalitarianism, 159

Ephesians, Ephesus, 87, 109, 117

eschatology, 45, 83, 160

Euodia, 139, 140, 146

Evangelical Free Church, 178

evangelical(s), evangelicalism, 10, 13, 14, 15, 21, 22, 26, 27, 28, 29, 30,

SCRIPTURE INDEX

ACKNOWLEDGMENTS

Every good book is a group effort, and I'm extremely thankful for the team of partners God has surrounded me with.

Many thanks to readers of the first draft of the book. I received helpful suggestions and faithful wounds from Mark Ward, Jim Berg, and Kevin Bauder—none of whom should be blamed for my final decisions. They would have written the book differently, I'm sure, but they were a help to me. Thank you!

Thanks to the friends who endorsed the book: Michael Barrett was a special encouragement to me. I needed his positive feedback. Thanks also to Andrew Bunnell, Phil Hunt, Sam Horn, Tim Keesee, Conrad Mbewe, Cary Schmidt, and Mark Ward. Endorsing a book like this, even if you're in agreement, takes some fortitude. I appreciate you!

As I mentioned in the dedication, Joe Tyrpak has thought through these issues with me for the last two decades. I owe him a great deal, not only for his influence on me but for his pastoring of my family when we served together at Tri-County Bible Church. It is no surprise that Joe's comments on the early drafts of this book were the most helpful I received. And as always, his design work for this book is on point. Thank you, Joe, for making time to make this book so much better.

Finally, the rest of the team at Church Works Media is a huge blessing to me. Thank you, Abby Huffstutler, for once again editing and improving one of my books. And thanks to Paul Keew, Scott Ashmore, and Peter Hansen for your work supporting and marketing the book. I'm so grateful for our crackerjack team, and I'm eager to see what the Lord allows us to do together in the future.

SDG! Grace!

Hymn-writer and experienced pastor Chris Anderson unpacks God's amazing gift of music and the role it can play in the life of every Christian. This book considers what Scripture says about the kinds of songs Christians should sing and helps believers choose them intentionally and objectively. It's also packed with extras, including small-group discussion questions!

"A thoughtful book bristling with biblical guidance, designed to help Christians worship God with theological depth and power."

—**Milton Vincent**, pastor, author of *A Gospel Primer for Christians: Learning to See the Glories of God's Love*

God is creating worshipers out of Samaritan women (like us) through the life-changing power of the gospel! John chapter 4 is a microcosm of what God is doing in the world, pointing us to answers for so many problems of our own day, such as racial prejudice, religious confusion, materialism, divorce, and sensuality. Join Chris Anderson on this study through his favorite narrative from Scripture, and find out how Jesus seeks, saves, and satisfies sinners.

"This book draws us into the conversation beside the well to see ourselves and, above all, to see the Hero of the story."

—**Tim Keesee**, author of *Dispatches from the Front: Stories of Gospel Advance in the World's Difficult Places*

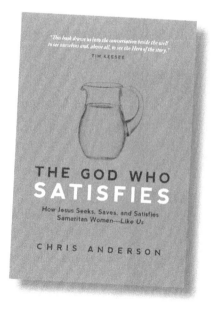

Gospel Meditations for Fathers

"This collection of thirty-one meditations is a must-read for any man striving to fulfill his God-given role as a father. Since each reading is both biblical and practical, it equips the reader to lead family members to greater love to Christ and to God's Word. As parents to four and grandparents to fifteen, Patricia and I recommend this as a fresh resource."

—*John MacArthur*

Gospel Meditations for Mothers

"In the midst of busy days and sleepless nights, moms need the encouragement that only the gospel can give. *Gospel Meditations for Mothers* offers powerful biblical truth and guidance that reminds moms of the importance of their labors and cheers them on in their daily tasks. Whether you're parenting a toddler or a teen, these gospel-focused reflections will minister to your heart as you care for your children."

—*Melissa Kruger*

Gospel Meditations for Young Adults

"*Gospel Meditations for Young Adults* is a breath of fresh air for young Christians and for all of us who are raising, discipling, mentoring, or just concerned about them and their spiritual growth and wellbeing. The devotionals are biblical, pastoral, succinct, readable, relevant, and relatable. More importantly, the focus is cross-centered and theological without being forced or trite. This would be a great tool to use in parenting, personal discipleship, group study, or even pastoral counseling."

—*Voddie Baucham*

Gospel Meditations for Prayer

"Brief and biblical, these meditations are full of sharp edges. They lead us to pray as cross-bearing disciples of Christ. Yet Anderson, Tyrpak, and Trueman comfort us with Christ's perfect grace for fallen people. So *Gospel Meditations for Prayer* is an encouraging book, but one designed to stretch you."

—*Joel Beeke*

Gospel Meditations for Christmas

"Too often Christmas speeds past us in a blur of busyness and stress, with only the briefest time and the shallowest thoughts given to the Christ that's meant to be at the heart of it all. Give yourself a Christmas to remember by using this profound devotional to pause, ponder, and praise our wonderful Savior."

—*David Murray*

Gospel Meditations on the Reformation

"Theologically rich, thoughtful, and historically rooted devotionals are a rare treat. This volume, which unfolds the theological commitments and pastoral heart of the Reformers, is a unique and enormously helpful devotional."

—*R. Albert Mohler, Jr.*

Gospel Meditations for Women

"Wrestling with guilt and frustration, far too many Christian women are living below the privileges of their spiritual inheritance. The solution is not found in any strengthened resolve of duty, but rather in having souls settled in the blessed liberty of Christ through the sweet enjoyment of the gospel. A union of sound doctrine and practical teaching, *Gospel Meditations for Women* beautifully highlights those unbinding messages of grace that so powerfully ignite joyful passion for Christ and holy living. What an invaluable resource!"

—*Holly Stratton*

Gospel Meditations for the Church

"We have come to expect meaty, edifying, superbly written devotional entries from Chris Anderson and his team. Here are thirty-one more, and they don't disappoint."

—*Phil Johnson*

Gospel Meditations for Missions

"Can we do missions without meditating on the gospel? Of course not. Yet, how many well-meaning, mission-minded saints go off into the harvest having failed to prepare their own hearts with due consideration of the good news? Too many I fear. *Gospel Meditations for Missions* helps us slow down to consider what is of first importance that we might hold this treasure more fully in our clay hearts."

—*Thabiti Anyabwile*

Gospel Meditations for the Hurting

"These meditations are Word-centered prescriptions that blow away the meaningless Christian platitudes often used to mask unanswerable pain. Until that day when Christ Himself wipes away all tears from our eyes, the Scriptures provide strength, help, and hope in this broken world. Let this book guide you to Christ, the only sure and lasting refuge."

—*Tim Keesee*

Gospel Meditations for Men

"Chris and Joe have co-authored a delightful and helpful little book of daily meditations. This is not one of those trendy Reformed 'the Bible says all men have to act like John Wayne or cavemen with better table manners' kind of productions. Many of the devotions are simply gospel expositions, and those which have a male-specific orientation are on topics like lust, where male psychology is important."

—*Carl Trueman*

Gospel Meditations on Creation

"Jeff Williams is a uniquely gifted human being whom God has put in extraordinary places. What is equally remarkable is how the wonder he finds in our Creator spills into all the ordinariness of the common day. I'd like to be more like that. In this devotional he and his fellow writers encourage us to just be amazed at the beauty and greatness of our Maker and Savior."

—*Keith Getty*